THE SURPRISE PARTY

THE GREATEST LOVE STORY EVER WRITTEN

A SELF-HELP AND MANIFESTATION GUIDE

B HARTVIGSEN

The opinions and characterization in this piece are those of the authors and do not represent any affiliation.

Copyright © 2020 B Hartvigsen
All rights reserved.

bhartvigsen75@hotmail.com

ISBN 978-1-7363110-0-4 (paperback)

Editing by Hayden Seder

Cover Design by Ana at 99designs

Formatting by ebookpbook

This book is dedicated to every individual that has been a part of my life's journey. You made this book come to life.

CONTENTS

CHAPTER 1	SURPRISE PARTY	1
CHAPTER 2	BELIEFS	5
CHAPTER 3	FATHER'S CHOICE	11
CHAPTER 4	A YOUTHFUL SETBACK	17
CHAPTER 5	FORGIVENESS	21
CHAPTER 6	CHILDREN	27
CHAPTER 7	SPIRALING DARKNESS	33
CHAPTER 8	REPROGRAMMING	37
CHAPTER 9	GOLF SLICE	43
CHAPTER 10	MONEY OWNERSHIP	45
CHAPTER 11	COMPLETE DESPAIR	53
CHAPTER 12	MORE SURPRISE PARTIES	57
CHAPTER 13	REMEMBERING DÉJÀ VU	59
CHAPTER 14	BREATHING	61
CHAPTER 15	BE PRESENT	67
CHAPTER 16	TRIATHLON	75
CHAPTER 17	MANIFESTATION	81
CHAPTER 18	LETTING GO OF THE PAIN	95
CHAPTER 19	LOVING YOURSELF	103
CONCLUSION		121

1

Surprise Party

I woke up from a beautifully surreal dream. In it, I was standing in front of an audience of beautiful people, speaking to them and thanking everyone for all the love that they have shown my loved ones and me. After finishing the speech, a few of the audience members came up to me. They lined up to commend me and give me love. I was embracing their love—it was so beautiful and gratifying! Then I woke up, lying in my bed as I recalled the vivid dream and tried to collect my thoughts. This was one of those dreams that felt so real that my current reality confused me. After a few minutes of thinking of the dream and all that had gone on in recent months, I suddenly imagined—as I had many times throughout my life—that today was the day! Today was going to be my surprise party! I sprang out of bed and hustled to get dressed, quickly brushed my teeth, and ran out the door, rushing to get to my car. I felt inspired to started driving to a place that I have often visited throughout my life; I drove to the cemetery where many of my family members are buried. Throughout my life I have pondered, prayed, and found peace in these hallowed grounds that hold a special place in my heart. As I drove, I could hardly contain my excitement that this was the day. Finally, *my* day.

LOVE YOURSELF

It was finally my surprise party! I rushed to get to the cemetery, imagining that everyone was going to be there waiting. My heart beat wildly at the prospect of finally seeing all my loved ones.

I pulled into the cemetery and drove down the lane, looking ahead for cars and a gathering of people. As I got closer to where my family members' plots are, I could see there was no one there. This surprise party was like all the other parties I had imagined throughout my life. I wanted to believe they would all be there, even though I knew it was just a story I had made up in my mind. I was instantly disappointed. I wanted to believe with all my heart that there was going to be a gathering of my loved ones there that day with party supplies and balloons, ready to shout, Surprise! when I drove up. It was going to be a celebration and a big party! This was not an ordinary surprise birthday party; it was going to be a surprise party to tell me all the trials I had endured in my life had been a test and that I had passed. The whole thing had been pre-planned to see if I would pass. They were all going to yell, Surprise, you made it and you passed the test!

Now I was here and the reality that no one would be there for me that day had set in once again. As I got out of my car and walked to my family's graves, I had tears in my eyes knowing, again, that today was not my surprise party like I had imagined my entire life. As I stood there and collected my thoughts and dried my tears, it all became clear to me: it *was* my surprise party that day, but a party for one. It was my day and I had finally passed all my life tests. I finally won! As I stood by the graves of my loved ones, I started to feel such gratitude and love. It was the day that I finally beat everything that

THE SURPRISE PARTY

I had gone through—years of pain, sadness, and hard work. After 45 years, I knew I finally loved myself.

Throughout my life, I had imagined these surprise parties, particularly after hard times or tragic incidents. I would visualize these parties over the years, their location and guests changing as my life changed. As I grew older, the party got larger. But I always imagined a big surprise party with everyone jumping out to yell, Surprise! Next, they would tell me it had all been a test and none of my hardship was real.

Along with my own hardships, I had a lot of family and close friends with hardship as well, something which only added to my sadness. I had always wanted to believe that the hard times were all just a made-up, fake, horrific opening act to a big surprise party.

But this time, it had happened. It was finally my surprise party, even though I was the only one in attendance. It was the best surprise party ever; it was beautiful. It had been 45 years since my birth, and it was finally my surprise party. It was the most magnificent day of my life.

As I sat there, pondering and crying with happiness to myself, I felt a complete and total love for myself. It was the first time in my life that I had ever felt love for myself. I finally felt worthy of love.

Looking back on my life, I have had numerous, beautiful stories. My life has been filled with many individuals who blessed me with their time and love. These beautiful souls have given me kindness and beautiful stories of love that are a part of who I am today. I want to tell you this book is the greatest love story ever written—the story of leaning to love myself.

2
BELIEFS

I want to start this book by telling you a few things: firstly, you are beautiful. And you are loved. Please repeat those two sentences to yourself. Know how beautiful you are and how deserving you are of love. Now if you set this book down and decide to never pick it up again or if you read it and only take away one small part from it, I want it to be just as I have said: You are loved and you are beautiful!

In my life, I have felt happiness and love, but I have also lived through plenty of times of darkness, fear, and hopelessness. I choose love and happiness and I choose to always give light and love. Doubts and fears are false, love is real. I pray that you will also know and choose to love as well. I hope this book will offer you a little light from any darkness you have felt.

I am a man of faith. I am a man who loves all faiths and teachings. I can honestly say that I am a member of all religions and faiths. I am spiritual, I am an Omnist. I am a human being that loves all human beings. I would personally wash the feet of any human being, as Jesus did his disciples. I would get on my knees and do just that to show you my love for you. I would personally hug and love anyone on this beautiful earth if he or she would allow it. You are all beautiful, loving souls to me.

Before I go further into the book, I want to let you know that I am going to refer to God a lot throughout. He will be referred to in this book by many names just as he is in this beautiful world. He is the forever loved one, he is the universe, our Dear Lord and Savior, the Heavenly Spirit, or Heavenly Father. God is our heavenly mother, our redeemer, Allah, or Christ the Lord. There are hundreds of different theological names that refer to God. I want you to know that my spiritual belief is that it does not matter what name you refer to him or her as; there is only one God and he is called many beautiful names. If you do not believe in a God—such as agnostic—then you still know there is the universe to believe in. Please believe in whatever you may want to call your higher power or the universe. All the divine beautiful names are true.

I believe that inspired men and women have been placed on this earth—both in the past and the present—by a higher power and the universe. I have love and respect for all their teachings. I have a great deal of love for the teachings of Muhammad, Buddha, Mother Teresa, and Christ, just to name a few, as well as the many hundreds of others who have been placed on this earth. They have all been sent to teach us love.

While writing this book, love and power came through me, not from me. I was inspired to write this book to teach others to learn self-love, insight, and guidance to a better life. I know there have been hundreds of books written regarding self-love and self-motivation. These books and teachings have relied on the message that if you think it, believe it, and manifest it, it will all come true. There have been numerous authors and a big movement spreading this message for the last twenty years. All of these are great teachings and inspired authors, are all correct. This book is just one more aid in helping you to find the truth of those teachings by sharing my own story on how I did this and how you can too. It all comes down to knowing self-love and believing. The meaning of life is within yourself, and you can know it by changing your mindset.

My life's journey taught me the four healing insights of reprogramming, forgiveness, letting go of pain, and loving yourself. The four healing insights are a guide to heal the areas of your life that may need it. This opened the door to the four discovery insights of money ownership, being present, breathing, and manifestation. The four discovery insights are tools to maintain physical and mental health for the rest of your life. Each one of the insights came to me through a different part of my life. These insights have freed me from the years of fears and doubts. They have also given me a beautiful life of peace, love within, and love for all. They have given me all my spiritual, financial, and professional wants and desires.

My hope is for you to implement the healing and discovery insights into your daily life. In doing this, they will give you all your spiritual, financial, and professional wants and desires. These insights will help you be a stronger and better you, should you choose to practice them.

I manifest to God and the universe that these teachings will help you have a more positive and blissful life. I know in my soul that if you work and put the time in by practicing these healing and discovery insights—or even just one of the insights—and work them into your life, it will be life-changing for you. You will be a better individual in all experiences throughout your life.

LOVE YOURSELF

As I look back at my life and everything that I have experienced—divine blessings, tragedies, loss, traumas—I can say that my life has not been more difficult than anyone else's. I want to emphasize this: My life has not been more difficult or harder than any other human being's. We have all faced sadness and damaging, hard times. But I can say as I look back at my life that it has been like a beautifully written book. There have been no wrong times. All the experiences I have had, have all been perfect and made me the beautiful person I am today. I am thankful and I am blessed!

The insights are not to help you through the grieving process. The grieving process has no exact formula, timeline, or presentation. I cannot tell you how to grieve or for how long. Please cry as hard as you want and for as long as you want; you know what is best for you. In my own life, I have dealt with all manner of death, suicide, divorce, lost love, physical trauma, and seemingly insignificant hardship such as bankruptcy and I have grieved over all the sadness and losses, sometimes crying for hours, weeks, or months on end. I share the story of my pain to show that I have an understanding of what you might be experiencing. I can only reiterate that I feel for you and I am praying that you find peace. Before starting these insights, take the time your heart desires to grieve and cry it all out. I would never want you to start practicing these insights without allowing yourself all the time in the world to grieve or to use these insights to fix or replace your grieving.

Your life trials are not what define you as the person you are today. Your life trials are not the real you. Your true self is the spirit and the love within your soul. The real you is who you were before all the trials of your life. We are all love.

The insights are life-changing strategies. As I explain these insights, remember that this book is just an introduction to these ancient practices. From these, you can then look further into each area and research their powers on your own. There are countless other books and teachings on these different practices; learning their powers is an endless voyage and the possibilities are endless. I encourage you to start looking deeply into each of them and learning all you can to enhance your life. I hope you have a new curiosity to search for more because there is more out there. These insights are not my own discovery, they are teachings from God and the universe that I am only giving a brief explanation of and how I have worked them into my life. These insights can be added to your personal beliefs— they are a simple addition to any religious belief. They are nothing more than an aid to becoming a more loving human being. By working through the four healing insights, you will free up your mind, giving you more peace in life and a more successful outcome with the four discovery insights.

Most of us have had internal challenges in life believing that we are not good enough or that we cannot achieve all we hope to. If you have not, then consider yourself extremely blessed or lucky. These insights will erase these fears and doubts. For the best results, I find it useful to use the insights as goals and write or type them out and hang them up where you will see them every day. These teachings are powerful and are not necessarily easy; they do require work! Depending on what your personal challenges are, some insights may be easier or harder than others. I can tell you that each one of these was difficult for me. It took time and reprogramming of my brain, something each of these insights will require.

I strongly encourage you to learn these practices, believe in them, write them down, and make them your powerful goals. Share them with your loved ones, both young and old. Incorporate them into your and their lives. You and your loved ones will be wiser in the face of possible trials and hard times you may face in the future. These insights will help you and them to grow young! I wish I would have known these insights earlier in my life. If I had learned them earlier, I know I would be a healthier person today.

These next chapters will be a blueprint to what helped me to regain my life again. Take care of yourself and your body while implementing these insights. Spoil yourself—you deserve it, you are worthy. And finally, be patient and show love to yourself through your healing journey. Healing yourself will be your greatest comeback in life.

As you read my life story, you'll see that there are many dark times and experiences that I was embarrassed by until I beat my own fears and doubts by applying the insights to my life. These insights inspired me to discover my own confidence and love toward myself. I am now at peace with myself and know I am an amazing human being. I am a survivor with a story to tell! I am no longer ashamed of who I am and the trials I have been given in my life. This is my story and I know I am not alone. I had wrongly programmed beliefs from my upbringing and was able to eliminate them by applying the healing and discovery insights. All my life trials and hardships led me to these insights which have made me who I am today. I manifest that these insights I am about to share will help you reach your full potential and achieve your desires and dreams.

3

FATHER'S CHOICE

Very few people know the stories contained in these next chapters. It is my hope that putting this personal information out there for all to read will help others.

To tell you my life story is to tell you how the healing and discovery insights played out through my life. I need to start at the beginning—the very beginning, 45 years to be exact. I was born to my beautiful mother, a woman with a heart of gold, into a family of three. She holds a special place in my heart and many other's. She is a hardworking and soft soul, a nurse that has achieved many accomplishments in her life. My mother was raised in a good, loving, religious family of cherry farmers. My grandmother was giving and nurturing as well as hardworking to name only but a few of her characteristics. I loved my grandmother with all my heart. My mother's father was a kind, hardworking farmer and the town cop.

My father was a hardworking man who was raised in a terrible and disruptive home, stories of which I've heard over the years. My father was raised by an angry, physically abusive man (my grandfather) while my father's mother was wonderful but simply too scared as a wife and mother to do anything to stop the abuse. That abuse helps explain the man who would become my father, a Navy Vietnam War vet and severe alcoholic with many of his own personal demons to fight. My father loved my mother, my older brother, and me with all his heart. He never physical hurt any of us; all he did was love and protect us. My father did have bouts of alcoholic delusions, but he was a hard worker and he loved us.

I have few memories of the first three years of my life though a few stick out, some good and some terrifying. I have a few memories of my father's alcoholic delusions and rages—though these events took place, I know my family and I were loved by my father. In fact, most of my memories are loving in nature and I am thankful for them giving me the love in my heart and passion that I have today.

One particular memory greatly influenced who I am today. I was just under the age of 4. This is the day that I started imagining the surprise parties. I grew up in a small city in an average neighborhood with people I am still friends with to this day. My mother was a stay-at-home mom with many responsibilities—one of them was Scouting Den Mother for my brother and his friends' scouting group is where they did outdoor activities for learning and achievement. Mom held the weekly scout meetings at our house for a lot of the neighborhood boys after school. After ending the meeting that day, one of the boys needed a ride home. This young boy, my mother, my brother, and I all loaded up in the family's 1968 yellow Blazer to take the boy home. After dropping him off, we drove back to our small three-bedroom home. We pulled into the driveway and unloaded, my brother and I quickly running into the house looking for our father. Dad had been on a drinking binge for days. The previous week, my father had lost a finger in a work-related accident due to a machinery malfunction. I followed my brother into the house and as I was running, I remember slowing down to look at the old wooden stereo console. I can still see it my mind. The stereo console was long with dark decorative wood and had a big lift lid on top. On the front of the console were two big, velvet, red speakers. As I walked by the stereo, I stopped to look at the record and noticed it skipping at the end of that side, making a scratching sound over and over. I then followed my brother to our parents' bedroom and just as we reached the bedroom door, my brother jumped from a loud noise. Instantly, everything stood still—time stopped. My brother turned around and ran back outside. Also scared by the loud noise, I followed my brother and ran out of the house.

That loud noise was the earth-shattering sound of a gun as my father took his life. My memories of the next few minutes are lost and don't pick up again until I'm crying on the corner of the city block, we lived just up the street from. I was standing with my brother and a good friend of my family's. This gentleman, who was also a father, had become a good friend of our family's and particularly a friend of my father's. My family and his have all remained friends over the years even after my father passing.

I only have vague memories of the days following my father's death. I can recall visiting the home of the man and his family who had stood on the corner that day. I also have small memories of my father's service and viewing. I have vivid memories of his funeral and the 21-gun salute given at all war veteran's funerals. My recollection of this moment is that it was very scary to me—the loud guns going off reminded me of my father taking his life. To this day, loud noises such as guns going off, balloons popping, and the odor of fireworks send me back to that day.

During the years after my father's passing, I had vivid dreams and would even daydream while in school of walking into my home after school and finding my father standing in the kitchen. As I walked in, my dad would turn and say, "Surprise! Surprise, it wasn't real, I never died!" He would always hug me and tell me I was safe and ok now.

After my father's death, I carried the experience close to my heart, even blaming myself for it. I felt he did it because of me. I felt he did not love me. I believed if he had loved me, he would have not done it. It was a big blow to my self-esteem at a young age, and I grew to dislike myself.

I remember being teased about my father's suicide in elementary school by a school bully and another neighborhood girl. It was embarrassing to me! I was always so embarrassed to have people ask me about my family members and subsequently ask about my father. I would then have to dreadfully tell them that my father was dead. It was terrible knowing that the next question would be: How did he die? I would have to tell them he shot himself then quickly leave the conversation with a knot in my stomach.

Growing up without my father was difficult, particularly when it came to typical father-son activities like camping and playing sports. I did have some exceedingly kind and special men in my life; male group leaders, family members, and my Grandpa all stepped up to do these activities with me. I am forever grateful to them and the example they set for me; however, it was still a self-esteem blow and uncomfortable to have to go to these events with them and not my father. My mom did her best to fill the role of both mother and father. She was my biggest fan at my sporting events.

My father's death left me with a changed outlook on life. It also instilled my own thoughts of suicide and preoccupation with death. I thought of suicide and death daily, weekly, monthly, and even by the minutes and seconds. When I experienced any difficulty like receiving bad grades, not getting asked to the dance, being teased, or anything that gave me feelings of failure or unworthiness, these suicidal and morbid thoughts rang through my mind. In addition to these suicidal thoughts, I thought of death all the time, both mine and my loved ones'. The thoughts of death could start with something as innocent as my mother going to the store and being gone too long. This was a time before cell phones when I could not just have called to see if she was ok. As I had these thoughts of death and suicide, I also visualized them. I saw the ambulance coming. I visualized the gruesome details. I saw every step of the event play out in my mind. I saw the burial and the family grieving and gathering. I saw my family member dead in a car wreck. These worries weighed heavily on me throughout my life and tormented me during my most trying times.

I can happily say I have stopped these thoughts and disrupted this "bad programming" in my life. I have sent the thoughts away and out into the universe; they are no longer in existence, something which I credit the healing methods in this book with.

4

A Youthful Setback

The next few years were a series of ups and downs. I had a loving mother that took on the duties of two parents and kept the family going. She started nursing school not long after my father's passing and graduated with her nursing degree when I was about 7. Later in life, my mother went on to receive a master's degree in nursing. Mom never remarried; I think my father broke her heart. She is an amazingly strong and beautiful woman. We stayed in the same small home for the next 18-plus years. My brother and I often stayed at our grandparents' home while growing up since mom was working and going to school. My grandparents' home was a loving home for us.

Around the ages of 4 to 6, I had a relapse of infantile incontinence. I was toilet-trained before my father's passing but after, fell back into a cycle of incontinence. This was very frustrating to me and my mother. My behavior was an embarrassing problem for me which I remember I just could not seem to fix. My mom would get very frustrated with me and when we went places, I was embarrassed that I smelled, and friends and family did not want to be near me. This was a big setback early in my life and another blow to my self-esteem at a young age. I felt terrible about myself. I told myself many terrible things: I stink, no one likes me, and I am gross. After going to numerous doctors for a diagnosis, it appeared that there was nothing medically wrong with me.

My mother tried taking me to a therapist, something one doctor had recommended. I can recall only going to see the therapist for just a few appointments, my mother always in the waiting room while I went in to talk. After a few appointments with this therapist, I attended one which was momentous, though what we discussed is vague in my memory. I remember sobbing uncontrollably and the counselor giving me a hug at the end of the session. Afterward, we walked out to greet my mother. As my mother and I left, I recall saying to her, "Mom, that was a bad meeting, that was not fun!" From that day forward, I never had another incontinence incident. I never went back to the therapist again. My problem was instantly fixed.

Later in life while speaking to a work colleague—a psychologist—I told him about my father's suicide and this setback it had given me. He explained that this event gave me such sadness and insecurities that it caused my young mind to feel I had no control of my life. This most likely caused the infantile incontinence. The mind does amazing things after trauma has taken place.

I would like to say for much of my life, and to this day, I have talked with a licensed therapist. The truth is therapy has saved me—I am a better person because of it. There is often a stereotype that going to therapy for help is "weak", but

THE SURPRISE PARTY

I am a 6'4", 275-pound "manly" man in my own opinion! I am not weak for seeing a therapist. This world would be a much better place if everyone spoke to a therapist; the benefits are astounding. Please reach out for help and meet with a licensed therapist. These beautiful, brilliant human beings are here to help us get through our struggles in life.

5

FORGIVENESS

The next few years of my life looked fine on the outside but inside, I felt terrible and deeply depressed. I was, to some extent, big for my age which led to being called mean names by my fellow elementary school classmates. This bullying made me believe I was fat, and I believed this when I looked in the mirror as well. I held this belief all the way into my late 30s. Looking back though, I was in no way close to heavy or fat. I find it remarkable that I was considered fat by other children. I know kids are mean, so I am glad to see the pendulum changing in our school systems nowadays to not allow bullying.

I was just starting elementary school when I was diagnosed with an acute case of dyslexia, a neurobiological learning disability characterized by difficulties with accurate and/or fluent word recognition and poor spelling and decoding abilities. There are different types of dyslexia learning disabilities; in my particular case, I would mix words and numbers entirely. This made simple spelling and writing as well as math extremely difficult. My disability required me to go to special learning classes in the mornings before school and sometimes after school, also attending summer school every year throughout elementary school. We had an exceptionally kind family friend that, by chance, was also one of my teachers in elementary school. This kind teacher would tutor me after-hours in reading and writing skills to overcome my learning disability. My mother would drop me off at my teacher's house before school for tutoring and then my teacher would take me to school with her. With this extra help, I was finally able to overcome my dyslexia. But my disability had left me behind in my schooling. I had to attend the resource special learning class all the way through high school, a class that teaches students with lessened learning accommodations. I even had special accommodations in my college courses. Unfortunately, this added to my already low self-esteem. I believed I was dumb, and I felt stupid. I remember one of my elementary school teachers making fun of me in front of the whole class for spelling a word wrong. The teacher and the whole class laughed and made fun of me. It was so embarrassing! I felt so terrible about myself. I told myself I was dumb and believed it for many years, even into my adulthood. I would mentally beat myself up with these thoughts time and time again.

By the time high school started, I appeared from the outside to be a good-looking, strong, somewhat-happy teenager. I played football and other sports and I had some close friends who I keep in contact with to this day. Internally, I did not think highly of myself and was constantly berating myself. On the outside, I tried to appear to be a tough teenager, but deep down I was still a scared little boy who just lost his father and was afraid of the world.

In high school I had a counselor who was good to me. I remember he would pull me into his office occasionally to check in on me and talk to me about my life. This was during a time when school counselors often spoke to students about personal life problems, something that seems to have gone by the wayside in our current school system. I had incredibly beautiful experiences talking to my counselor. He and another school counselor teamed up and counseled me regarding my father's passing. These sessions were extremely helpful and life-changing for a struggling teenager. The counselors would call me out of class a few times a week for counseling sessions in their office. During the few weeks we spent together, we talked a lot about my father's death. Those sessions changed my perspective—up until then, I had always blamed myself for his death. The counselors got me to consider that, in my father's mind, he was helping me by taking his life. My father thought that he was no good for us and that killing himself was ultimately a favor to us. I had lived with that false shame all my life. The low self-esteem I had suffered from over the years from the guilt I felt finally started to lift; it was not an instant change, but it was a relief in my outlook on life and my perception of myself.

At this time in my life, I began to learn the first healing insight of forgiveness. Forgiveness is an immensely powerful insight. Every person that crosses our path throughout our life journey, whether during good times or trying times, is a part of our healing journey. There are no mistakes in life, only lessons to be learned. By forgiving and healing from your past, you will be set free. By forgiving yourself and others you receive inner peace.

There are two parts to the forgiveness insight. The first part is forgiving others for their role in any difficulty and pain they caused you. I will get to the second part of the forgiveness insight later in the book.

LOVE YOURSELF

The first part of the forgiving insight is forgiving others who have caused you pain or sadness. Many of us have traumas, sadness, or pain in our lives that we had no active role in; we were merely a recipient of these hardships. I would like for you to ask yourself whether you have any anger toward anyone in your past. This could be a parent, family member, or it could be even someone you only met just for a moment in your past. If a person has willfully caused you pain and sadness, they also have pain within. While working on myself, I started working on forgiving others for their role in the difficulty, sadness, and pain that I experienced.

I needed to find forgiveness for the pain and sadness that was caused by my father. I also had no ownership in this pain, but this was a big one for me to battle through. I have done a lot of therapy throughout my life over this heartbreaking event. Later in life, I was encouraged by a therapist to write a letter to my father to find forgiveness. I wrote a letter to my father explaining to him how he hurt me and how much pain he had caused me. This pain and sadness still affect me, even today. In the letter, I wrote about how much pain he caused my family. I told him of my frustration that I had to pick up and take care of his responsibilities that he left behind. I also let him know how he helped me to become a better person from his actions. I am a better person because of his decisions. At the end of the letter, I was then able to let go of the pain he had caused me. I took the actual letter and dug a small hole and buried it. I have also heard of burning the letter and letting the ashes fly away. This symbolizes letting them and your past pain go as the ashes all drift away. The burying of the letter was a great way for me to release all the sadness and pain I had endured. By doing this, I was able to start to heal and move on in life.

My high school years were filled with good memories and bad memories like any teenager experiences; I was asked to a few dances and I was also turned down on a few dances. I had never been kissed nor did I dare to. I never had a girlfriend. I felt I was not attractive. I had exceptionally low self-esteem regarding my looks and mentality.

Just two weeks before graduation, I was required to go on a high school survival trip. This five-day campout in the wilderness was intended to teach us learning skills and team-building. The trip was put on by the high school and the two counselors that helped me were the trip leaders. This was for a select group of kids; if I did not go, I wouldn't be able to graduate—my grades were holding me back. I figured, why not go? It's camping, it's outdoors, and it'll be more fun than being in school. I signed up and ended up learning a lot about myself. I also made a friend on that trip who would have a huge impact on my life.

With a lot of help from my mother and her pushing me constantly to work hard, I graduated. I have always said that my mother should have been the one that walked across the stage on my graduation day.

6

CHILDREN

On that high school survival trip, I made a new friend by the name of Laura; she was a dream! She was the first girl that actually paid attention to me and smiled back at me. I had never noticed her before that trip. I didn't even know she existed, but it turned out we had been in the same class together all through school. She was a quiet girl, and I was this loud, obnoxious boy trying to convince everyone I was someone grand. I remember when I first saw her on that survival trip at this beautiful waterfall. We were all swimming and having fun. I was instantly in love. I knew she was the girl of my dreams. As it turns out, I would end up having four beautiful boys with that girl. We had some beautiful times and some very trying and growing times together—many of which were due to me being unhealthy. We were two young, immature kids who believed we needed to make it permanent. We thought we knew what love was and that this was what one did after graduating: find the girl of your dreams and get married. Wow, I needed to grow up a lot. But that is what we did. We dated for a few years after graduation and then we got married. Looking back, I would not change a thing about our relationship and our time together. I learned a lot, but my insecurities did not help the relationship and our time together was not healthy.

Then we had our first beautiful baby boy; he was perfect. I love this cute little boy with all my heart and soul. I had a fairly good job as an electrician which, over time, I had grown to be quite successful at and provided somewhat well for our family. Our relationship always seemed to struggle, and my self-esteem issues did not help with this. I was quite a mess at that time in my life, drinking heavily and feeling down on myself. I had started drinking right out of high school; I had just never really grown up or let go of the childhood traumas that I endured mentally. The drinking did not help, it just brought me down more slowly before eventually catching up with me. One day, I was drinking heavily, and I dropped our baby boy. He was not hurt, but I felt terrible; I had failed as a parent. There are a lot of events from my alcoholic years that I am ashamed of and while those shames have made me who I am today, they are nevertheless embarrassing to look back on.

In addition to drinking heavily, my wife and I were fighting all the time. I had gotten really intoxicated one day and decided I was going to do exactly what my father did and take my life with a gun. I was very combative, and my wife decided enough was enough and with the help of some of my family, they checked me into a rehab program. This was extremely embarrassing for me and a direct hit to my pride; I felt like a bad father and husband and an absolute embarrassment to my family. If I remember right, I was in rehab for about a week. I needed to quit drinking and I agreed to get some counseling. After I checked out of rehab, I stopped drinking for about a month or so but slowly slipped back into my old ways and managed to keep my problem hidden for quite some time. After work, I would stop just down the road from our house and quickly have a drink before going home. I would then distance myself from my wife, so she did not smell it on me and suspect I was drinking again.

I did uphold my agreement to get some therapy. I will never forget one particularly life-changing therapy session. I remember it like it was yesterday. My therapist and I were discussing my wanting to take my life. My counselor stopped me during the session and had me look outside. She wanted me to realize what I had and who I was. She wanted me to see the beauty in this world. I recall the office had some big picture windows looking out on a stunning mountain view. To this day, I do not know what she said or what changed in my thinking, but my mindset shifted dramatically in that moment. I completely changed my relentless need to take my life. The ongoing, agonizing thoughts in my mind completely stopped! I realized that I strongly did not want to take my life. I wanted to live! In fact, I would have been quite angry at God if he were to ever take me in an accident or illness. I walked out of that session that day a changed man.

But I was still hiding my very problematic drinking. I finally confessed to my wife that I had been drinking. I carried my new will to live for probably two-plus years. I was still drinking and had not changed my stance on it, but I knew I did not want to die now. It was fantastic that the voices in my head had stopped. My life looked good, so I thought.

Not long after that, we had two beautiful twin boys whom I love with all my soul. I was building our second home and it was a really good time in my life, aside from the drinking—I was doing well at my job and we were having fun as a family. About a year after the twins were born, my partner told me that she was pregnant again. What a shock! To our brood of three beautiful boys, we added a fourth boy who I love with all my heart.

What a magnificent gift my four boys are to me. My boys have taught me a love that has made me a better person in all aspects of my life. After our fourth was born, life started to change quite severely for myself and my wife. I can remember sitting in a recliner one evening holding three little crying babies and the fourth little boy playing in the bedroom. It was intense! Three little babies screaming and crying in my arms! I remember thinking, what I am doing? There were lots of insecurities going through my mind. My wife and I were still not getting along, and we had grown apart over the years. Our fighting and my drinking and insecurities led to an unhealthy relationship and we ultimately decided to end it. It was a heart-breaking decision, but I was drinking a lot and spiraling downward.

Though we ended up parting ways, my partner was and is an incredible woman and mother. She is an extremely kind soul to everyone. Despite our differences, I did love her or at least what I knew love to be at that time in my life. I thank her for sharing with me her four beautiful boys and her time and love.

The separation brought up a lot of self-esteem issues within me. I was devastated and had many days and nights of crying. I started to question everything: Why was I not good enough? Was it a sexual thing? Am I not man enough? I was once again having thoughts of taking my life. I started to tell myself my boys would be better off. The suicidal thoughts increased as I constantly berated myself. I am not sexy! I must be gross! I am a bad guy! I am not a good provider! I am a bad dad! It was a terrible time, mentally beating myself up. My abandonment issues that I had already formed at a young age played into all my separation fears. I lost a sense of security I had had for years and felt I could never trust letting someone in again. I started to build up big walls, never letting my guard down and building them higher and higher.

7

SPIRALING DARKNESS

After the separation, I moved out of our home and into a little one-bedroom apartment. My four boys and I stayed there for some time after the divorce. I had decided I needed to quit drinking, but this only lasted for about six months due to my low self-esteem and the pressure I was under. The boys went back and forth between both their mother's and my home. I moved onward and built myself a little home.

I started drinking quite heavily again at this time in my life. I really went downhill drinking. I was extremely tormented with my thoughts and my self-esteem.

I became incredibly angry and lost after losing what had once been an extremely strong faith in a higher being. I had always believed in prayer and a God, so much so that I believed God could move mountains. Before our separation, I believed God could fix our failing relationship. I remember praying and praying to him to fix us. I look back at how I was so believing that he could fix us, but I wasn't looking at myself as what needed to be fixed. It is up to us to be healthy and loving. I knew and believed our redeemer could bring my partner and I back together. I just knew he could! I believed it with all my heart! I prayed so hard and, of course, it did not happen.

I was single for about two-plus years. I was Godless and an angry alcoholic, bitter toward God for not fixing my relationship. As I questioned his role in my failure, I began to ask why God would let my brother and me walk into our house to find our father taking his life. Why couldn't he have just led us to a friend's house to play? We did not need to witness that horrific event that would haunt us our entire lives! I questioned where God was often during these times. I questioned where God was for those suffering from heartache and depression, where was he with all the destruction in the world? I was so angry at God! I became so hateful and bitter toward him. I knew that he did not exist; I hated him! I despised him! This time of my life was a dark and sad time without God. I was still holding my job and being a responsible father to my four boys. It was during the afterhours of being a dad when they were asleep or not with me when I was a drinking wreck. I was living the most Godless, fearless life.

Many of my drinking binges ended with me in places I didn't know, or not knowing how I got there. I would wake up at bars and other places with unhealthy people. Looking back on those years now gives me chills at some of the horrible places I ended up. The drinking and subsequent drugs were a big problem. My soul was Godless and angry, and I was so depressed and drinking even more. Despite this, the added drugs and alcohol fed my ego, making me feel confident and grand. I was drinking more and more, feeling good about myself, going out dancing and partying, and living a bachelor life after the hours of being a father. I was also working a different job and doing well financially. But looking back, I was so obviously an insecure, sad person.

I had been living this way for roughly two years when I met Stacy. Meeting her was a major event in my life. We dated for a little more than a year, constantly partying and feeding into an unhealthy relationship. And of course, I felt she was *the one*. I felt it was time to give her a ring! What a mess that relationship and I were. We got engaged—I thought I knew what love was and that I was happy. In reality, I was a sinking ship and drinking uncontrollably most of the time. My fiancée saw this dark side of me and confronted me about it. I told her I would never stop drinking and that I had everything under control, like I had numerous times before in my life. With that, she brought back the engagement ring I gave her. I was devastated and embarrassed. I believed she made me a much better person, once again thinking that happiness and health could be found outside of myself. We went our separate ways, though I (unsuccessfully) tried to get her back which ended up being a blessing in disguise. Today I am thankful she was the strong one and could see that my lifestyle was unhealthy and would only bring us both down.

8
REPROGRAMMING

After our breakup, I could finally see all the harm my addictions were causing. I had finally hit rock bottom and decided that I had ruined enough of my life and that of my four boys. My alcoholism had caused major problems in my first relationship, led to the end of my last relationship, and caused undue stress to my family members, especially my mother. My mother's heart was breaking to watch me continue in my father's footsteps. I did not realize it at the time, but my drinking had been the cause of my self-esteem problems and many insecurities. I knew it was time to finally quit drinking and quit drinking for good. Over the years, I had tried time and time again to quit. I would go on a bad drinking and drug binge and wake up the next morning promising to be done. I would throw all my alcohol in the garbage can. In those instances, I was completely committed to quitting drinking but, of course, I would wake up a few days later and start drinking again, hoping it had not been garbage pickup day yet so I could get all the bottles back out of the garbage can. What a mess I was!

This time though, things were different. I dumped everything out and I finally knew that I needed to change. It was one of the hardest things I have ever done. I went out and bought a mountain bike to keep me busy and to stop the alcohol cravings. I remember riding until my lungs felt as though they would burst. Exercise seemed to be the only thing that could keep my mind off the dreadful desire to drink again. I would go for long rides, just pedaling as hard as I could—anything I could do to stop the drinking thoughts even for just one minute. The temptations were so terrible that sometimes I would sit on the couch crying my eyes out, trying anything imaginable to curb the desire to drink. One time, I bought a bottle of alcohol and sat on my couch holding it, debating in my head whether to just start drinking again. In the end, I held strong and dumped it out.

With the voices in my head constantly telling me to drink again, I felt so helpless and at such a loss that I decided to kneel and pray. Let me remind you that at this time I did not believe in a God and if there was a God, I hated him! Why would I fall to my knees and pray if I did not believe? This so-called God was never there for me. Despite these feelings, I decided that it might be the only thing I could do to help stop the temptations. The voices were so overwhelming, it was like a war going on in my head. I remember praying with all my heart, sobbing in tears to please take the temptations away. *Please God! Please! Please take away the wars going on in my head!* I prayed and prayed with all my soul. After a few hours, the voices started to let up. It was helping, it was really helping! I prayed more and more. The voices and wars were easing up. I did this for weeks and it was working! I prayed hourly. When I was at work and the cravings would start, I would need to immediately find a quiet place—even just a bathroom stall—and kneel and pray. After a few months of this, I was no longer drinking, and I was starting to find some peace.

One day, everything suddenly clicked. I had stopped drinking and was still needing to pray hourly throughout the day, but it was working. I don't remember exactly where I was, but I remember watching the sunset one evening and my life changed completely. I had lived in this dark existence all my life but had suddenly seen a new light.

Prayer had let me finally see God's beauty in this world. When my eyes were opened to a new, God-loving, sober life, I saw the sunset that evening and a new understanding in my new, beautiful life. My life up until that sunset had been like a black-and-white televised world; after that sunset, my heart and my vision opened up, instantly turning my life to color. It was like the scene in *Wizard of Oz* when Dorothy walks through her house. Up until that point in the movie, everything had been shown in black and white. As she opens her front door and walks out into the new land of Oz, everything in the new world turns to the most vibrant, beautiful colors. From that point on, the rest of the movie is in full color. That was how my life changed that evening. My life felt so brilliant! This was a complete and total change in my outlook on life. I now loved God!

I was so happy and so thankful! I was alive, everything had color, everything was beautiful! I was not drinking, and I was on top of the world! The sunsets and sunrises were the most gorgeous, beautiful events I had ever seen! I was so emotional, and I realized that I had barely cried in my life. But I had turned into this new, emotional, happy, beautiful guy. I cried at everything! I cried at the sunsets and I still do. I have done this for years. I cried at how beautiful everything and everyone is. I cried at my four beautiful little boys! It was the most divine, happy time of my life! This was my most life-changing moment, a new life—a rebirth.

It was during this time of my life that I started to learn the second healing insight of reprogramming. We are all programmed by beliefs at a young age. Some beliefs are good and healthy while others are less so. This programming might include traditions, religious beliefs, how we act and treat others, and even little simple ways of life such as how we cook, how we clean, how we eat, and how we work. Some of these programmed beliefs are right for us and continue to benefit our lives and some do not work and are outdated. Your programming stems from past generations—your parents had programming from your grandparents, your grandparents had it from their parents and so on. Your programming can go as far back as four to five generations from our ancestors.

Here is a story about a newlywed couple that gives you an idea of how our programming makes its way into our lives. This cute newlywed couple are ecstatic to be starting a new life together in their new home. The two go to the store for the first time together and the new bride has decided that she wants to cook their first Sunday dinner together. She is so excited to be doing this for him! While at the store, she proceeds to buy a roast and potatoes, carrots, and all the fixings to go with it. She wants to make this perfect, just the way her mother always did when she was growing up. Sunday comes along and she excitedly starts to get ready for their first Sunday dinner together. Her husband excited as well. She unwraps the roast, sets it on the cutting board, and cuts off the corner of the roast and throws it away. The new husband is confused as he sees her doing this and asks, "Why did you cut the corner of the roast off and throw it away?" "That is how my mother did it," she tells him. "It makes the roast that much better; it cooks better in the juices." After the roast cooks and simmers for most of the day, everything turns out perfect! They have their first Sunday dinner together, and it is a perfect first little newlywed Sunday dinner.

A few weeks go by and they decide they are going to go to Sunday dinner at her family's house. While there, her mom is making a big Sunday dinner for the whole family. She asks her mother why cutting the corner of the roast off makes it more tender and juicier. Her mom smiles and tells her that she did not cut the roast off to make it taste better, she simply cut the roast off because the only pan that she owned would not fit that big of a roast.

This story is just a small example of how our programming is passed down to each of us by our lineage. It is your responsibility to look at the different programmed beliefs instilled in you from birth and decide if they are healthy or not in your healing journey. It is your responsibility to break those unhealthy programmed cycles.

I promise you that if you heal and stop or change these unhealthy programmed patterns in your life and stop teaching them to your children and family, you will clean up generations of unhealthy patterns. I am not going to say that all programming is wrong; we do have beautiful programming in us all. This healthy programming has made us beautiful in our own way. It is your choice to really look at your life and see if the life patterns you have adopted suit you in your daily life.

I am going to give you the secret of life. This is huge! Are you ready? The secret to life is changing your mind and reprogramming it to a positive mindset. Reprogramming your mind to not have addictions, reprogramming your mind to only allow successes, or reprogramming your mind to a new life you want. You will face many hard obstacles in your life and, after all is said and done, it all comes back to reprogramming your magnificent, beautiful mind to a healthier outcome.

I was programmed in many wrong ways from my childhood as many of us are. I was programmed to believe that alcoholism is a way of life. I was programmed with battling the debilitating shame and thoughts to always end my life. Looking back at some of the lowest times in my life, I was always struggling with my self-esteem. I felt like I was unwanted by my family. I had nothing within me, I believed I was not worthy of love. The voices ran through my mind, screaming at me to take my life and to finally end things. The voices would start, and I would visualize it taking place. I've had to reprogram my mind many times throughout my life to completely do away with all these wrong thoughts.

9
Golf Slice

I was living this new life for only a few months when a good friend told me about this girl named Sadie that he thought I should go out with. I agreed and got her number from my friend and finally decided to text her. We started texting back and forth, slowly building a beautiful new friendship. We texted for a week or two, just asking each other random questions about who we are, what we liked, and our beliefs. I loved her answers, and I was excited by all our previous texts and topics we had discussed. I knew I wanted to meet her. We met and there was an instant connection. We had a lot in common and a lot of the same beliefs. I started to fall for her even more and felt so happy and excited with myself and my new life. Quitting drinking, finally swallowing my pride, and falling to my knees had changed everything about my life. His Holiness changed my life. I am sober! I promised God I would remain sober because of his love for me. I promised him I would do or go through anything he gave me to prove my love to him. I felt I owed God my life and soul for giving me a new life. Those dark years had been a test, but I had held on and beat them all. Now it seemed that not only had God given me a new, beautiful, sober existence, he had also blessed me with the most gorgeous woman ever.

Sadie and I were instantly best friends. We did everything together. She had five beautiful little ones, ranging in age from 4 to 15. I grew to love her children and still love them to this day. It was quite a beautiful time in my life. We dated and we had a lot of fun. I remember going golfing for the first time with her. Over the years, I had picked up a bad slice with my golf game. For those who don't know what a "slice" is, it is when you hit the ball and the ball automatically pulls to the right. It is a bad problem and hard to fix. While we were hitting balls on our first golf outing, my first ball went straight as an arrow. I had no idea why, but I joked that she had changed me and fixed my golf swing instantly. This girl was beautiful and fun. Our lives were so exciting together. We did things together with our kids—quite a crowd between her five children and my four boys. Everything was simply perfect. We got serious and continued dating for another two years before deciding to start a small coffee shop business together. I was a general contractor, building homes and doing well financially while she ran the coffee shop. We were on top of the world and everything was beautiful and perfect. I remember questioning at times whether I had died because I felt like I was in heaven. We had many special times and many spiritual times together.

10

MONEY OWNERSHIP

Of the many spiritual events I have had in my life, there is one I choose to share for its effect on my life. Sadie and I were driving home one evening and exited the freeway to the little town where we lived. As I turned onto the freeway off-ramp, I suddenly had this overwhelming déjà vu unlike any I had ever experienced. It was so overwhelming, even scary, that I turned to Sadie and said, "I am having this very intense déjà vu." Her eyes lit up as she responded that she was also having intense déjà vu. At this point it was getting overwhelming. I had had déjà vu before quite a few times in my life, but nothing like this. Déjà vu is associated with temporal lobe epilepsy. This experience is a neurological anomaly related to epileptic electrical discharge in the brain, creating a strong sensation that an event or experience currently being experienced has already been experienced in the past. For many including myself, déjà vu can be described as a somewhat fun feeling like you have been there and done that before. If you look at these events from a spiritual standpoint, a lot of individuals do believe that maybe in another lifetime you have been there and done that before. It is a familiar feeling like you are finally at home. Some people have never experienced déjà vu, but the individuals that have known that feeling know it to be quite real.

To experience déjà vu with someone else simultaneously is exceedingly rare. Déjà vu generally only happens for a second or two, even a flash of a moment. Our mutual déjà vu began as we drove on the off-ramp, but it continued as we drove on. It started to scare us how long it was lasting. Finally, I spoke up and said, "Did we get in a car wreck and die? What is going on?" We both were a little bit fearful! I decided to pull over to figure out what was going on. We drove until we found a little driveway to pull into, a small spot entering a cemetery—an odd place to stop considering what was taking place. We stopped and sat there talking and wondering what had taken place. As we talked, the déjà vu finally ended.

We talked about that experience over the next few years as a divine moment in our lives together. This was an event that was personal and spiritual to us. We believed it was a spiritual moment where God told us that we were good together. We felt we were two people who God had brought together for a reason. It was a beautiful, spiritual experience that I will never forget.

We continued dating, going on exciting adventures with our kids and generally having a fun time in our lives. In 2008, I was doing well financially, and everything felt so spiritually aligned and perfect. We knew that we were destined to be together. We felt Allah gave us each other. I bought her a ring one day and asked her to marry me in my walk-in closet. Not the most romantic place to propose, I know, but I was so excited. And she was so excited. It was beautiful. I had built this home and we had agreed that it would be the perfect home to

THE SURPRISE PARTY

live in and join our families together after we were married. She said yes and agreed to marry me.

Both of us felt on top of the world; we had everything going for us. Not too long after becoming engaged in 2008, a global recession devastated the world financial markets as well as the banking and real estate industries. The crisis led to increases in home mortgage foreclosures worldwide and caused millions of people to lose their life savings, their jobs, and their homes. Home loans had become out of control as banks over-loaned to underqualified people leading to homeowners defaulting on their mortgages. It was a big mess. I had owned and built many rentals and was starting construction on a smaller commercial project (though a larger one for me as an independent contractor). The project was a few doctor's office buildings. Suddenly the housing market fell out and the economy fell into a recession. There were no loans being given out. I went from being in a particularly good financial situation to making no money whatsoever. This completely turned my life around. Suddenly, the little coffee shop that my partner and I started together provided our only income and it was barely surviving. It was only meant to be a little side business, and it was just breaking even in that first year it had opened—good for a startup business, but I had previously been keeping it afloat with my construction business. Everything started to fall out from under us. My fiancée also had a home she owned and was losing it. I was instantly losing all my rentals and the home we were going to live in. I was also losing the commercial project I was just starting.

This was a trying time; it was devastating to be losing everything I had worked for over the years. I was blessed to have family close by so my boys and I moved in with them. This was so terrible and depressing. My mind began running wild with negative thoughts about myself: I was a failure and no good! I believed I was nothing. I believed my money made me who I was. My thoughts of suicide were running rampant. I was struggling to feed my kids. We moved my partner into a tiny basement apartment after she lost her home. It was not fair to her or any of us, but I was losing the beautiful home that I had built for us to join families together. We were losing everything and with all the stress we decided to break things off between us and go our separate ways. What had once felt like paradise had turned to a hellish nightmare. Talk of joining two families of nine children together is intimidating with no income. We had only been broken up for a few weeks when we agreed to make it work and get back together. We decided we did love each other, and we were going to get married; we would just work hard and make it work. We got married in a beautiful ceremony on a stunning fall day on a small mountain top overlooking the valley we lived in.

At the time, I was out of a job in the construction industry, an event that led to me finding a new life-changing career working with the mentally ill. My new role was essentially as a CNA (Certified Nursing Assistant) at a state mental institution, a place I have grown to love with all my heart. I was making $9.41 an hour there, quite a change from a general contracting salary and difficult to provide for a family of 11 on. Going from construction to bathing patients was completely eye-opening and a big lesson in humility.

Working with this population has truly been a blessing; they teach and give me so much more than I teach or give them. These beautiful patients are survivors who have been tormented and traumatized due to their conditions. My heart goes out to all that fight mental illness and what they go through in life. My heart also goes out to their families. It is hard for families to understand mental illness and be able to help their loved one. I am so thankful that I was forced this direction in my career and life.

My wife had also decided to close the little coffee shop and come work at the mental institution as well. She was also doing the same line of work as I. With her and I working and having finally gotten married, we moved our family of 11 into a small three-bedroom home. The home was a little restricted. It was a lot of life changes, all within six months. With all that was going on, she and I began to grow apart; we had lost everything, were living together with nine little kids, and working graveyard shifts. Things were tough mentally, physically, financially, and emotionally. Sadie was not happy. Once we had gotten married, she had become quite sad and unhappy. I was not too happy myself and had low self-esteem once again. After about a year, we decided that maybe we needed to start thinking about breaking up.

At this time in my life was when I started to learn the first discovery insight of money ownership, something I had difficulty learning at first. I struggled with money over the years and that struggle developed into self-punishing jealousy. Once I incorporated this insight into my life, I realized its truth and its power to make all your worldly desires come to you. I had to learn to believe in it, know it, feel it, see it, and even taste it, if that is possible. Once I achieved this insight, my life started to change, not only in terms of the abundance of money but the peace behind it as well. There is plenty of wealth to go around! Once you believe this powerful insight with all you have, you will also see that there is plenty for all!

Before finding this insight, I was extremely jealous about money—who had it and how much they had. This was a time when I *thought* I had nothing. When I say jealous, I mean that I was angry jealous! I spent years fighting over money and telling myself I had none. I was also doing therapy with a fantastic and very enlightened therapist at the time. I was discussing my hang-ups in life over money with her and how I had always felt jealous, left out, or picked on when it came to money and finances. Why does my neighbor Fred have it so good and so easy? He has everything! Always asking myself, why do I have it so hard and have nothing? Why is he making good money and I am not? Why is he able to buy whatever he wants, the boat, truck, nice home? I became more and more jealous over the years. As I was telling my therapist about my neighbor, she asked me something I will never forget: Whose money is it? I paused and thought about it. She asked, Is it your money? I answered, Yes, it is my money! She asked, Is Fred's money his money? I answered yes again. No, she explained, it is not your money and it is not Fred's money. It is God's money. God owns everything in the world and in the universe. *God and the universe own all the money!*

Well, that took me by surprise. I thought to myself, *Wow, that is deep! I have never really thought about it that way!* I knew that this is all God's and the universe's world, and we are all God's creation, but I never thought about it in those terms. God and the universe do own everything. It is a simple and easy concept. It is all God's and the universe's money. We do not own one thing other than our freewill. For most of us, we do not even own the cars and homes we have and enjoy; in most cases, the bank owns them. But in all truth, it is all owned by God. God owns the home, the bank, and the kitchen table. The Heavenly spirit owns it all! If you are agnostic, it is all owned by the universe.

I started to really think about this and believe in it. It is a beautiful truth, and it was huge for me, life-changing. My previous thoughts and negative emotions toward money and life all started to change. I was starting to believe it. I started to humble myself knowing that I do not own one thing out there. It is all God's! It is all God's money! Everything I have ever had to this day was always owned by God.

If you can believe that it is all God's and know that it is truly not yours—believing it with all your soul—then the next step is changing your vocabulary when referring to what you thought you owned. I still catch myself saying I own something, but I am getting better at it. Once you have changed your vocabulary, your life will completely change. It will be a new outlook on life. It is all owned by God, God simply loans it to you. God allows us to borrow and enjoy all her beauties in this world. God wants you to have all your needs and desires and she wants you to enjoy her gifts. You are deserving of all of it! All you are to do is simply enjoy the wealth. Enjoy God's house, God's car, God's swimming pool, etc. You only have three obligations: be extremely grateful for the gifts, pray over the gifts, and celebrate the gifts! The money is all God's—receive it, thank him, and then let it go with gratitude and know it is all coming back double and even triple to you.

I encourage you to reprogram this insight into your mind. It is a hard one, but I can tell you it is the truth. As soon as you conquer this goal, all that is in God's world will flow to you. And finally remember to tell yourself how perfect you are and how beautiful you are while you are practicing this insight.

11

COMPLETE DESPAIR

Sadie and I started talking about splitting up. We were trying to make things work, but it was touch-and-go as we struggled back and forth. It was hard with all that had gone on and both she and I working graveyard shifts certainly didn't help—working at those hours makes you feel like you're living in a completely different realm. I know there is a special place in heaven for all people in this world that work graveyard shifts. It is extremely taxing on the body, both mentally and physically. These beautiful keepers of the night keep this world running when the rest of the world is sleeping soundly. They are a blessing to us all. I say thank you! Between all our life changes and trying to keep our children healthy and happy, we just could not catch a break.

One afternoon Sadie and I were driving home. We happened to be off work on the same day, a rare occurrence. My wife was not doing so well. She was very unhappy with us and our life. We had decided to go for a car ride like we had done many times before. Our ride was getting to the end, so we headed home. On our way home as we were getting off the freeway of the little town we lived in, my wife's phone rang. She did not know the phone number, so she chose not to answer it. A few seconds later my phone rang, and it was the same number. I also did not answer it, not knowing the number. Then the same phone number called on my wife's phone again. She said out loud, "That is strange." Then suddenly, my phone rang again. This time I knew the number calling was my work which was odd since they usually did not call me. I said, "I will just let them leave me a message." Right after that, her phone rang again; it was our work calling her. She said out loud, "I guess I will answer the phone, someone is trying to get ahold of us." She answered the phone to the most horrific news. It was a doctor from our work informing her that there had been an incident with her boy at our work. My wife's oldest son had a job as a helper for the cooks in the kitchen at the same institution where both Sadie and I worked. As I drove up this long, straight road from the freeway, I listened to my partner talk on the phone and then suddenly let out the most horrific scream anyone could ever hear. The scream still vividly stands out in my mind; I will never forget it. I pulled the car over into a little turn-off to a small cemetery, the same spot we had pulled over during our episode of déjà vu, the coincidence and synchronicity of which we would not realize until later. The doctor told Sadie that her son had tried to take his life in the bathroom while at work. To listen to a mother, hear this news about her son is the most heart-wrenching sound in the world.

I immediately turned the car around and drove to the hospital, about a ten-minute drive away. I hardly even remember the drive aside from my partner calling a couple of her family members on the way. There was so much confusion and turmoil. We arrived at the hospital to find a hospital social worker waiting for us to inform us that the paramedics were unable to revive her son. It was truly one of the most heartbreaking moments of my life. He was just 19 years old. He was an extremely cute boy and my partner's pride and joy. He had graduated high school, was working, and even talking about going to college. We thought everything was going well for him in his life.

After the news, I don't remember much—it was all quite surreal and incredibly sad. One moment that does stand out was the emotional difficulty of getting my wife's other small boys dressed and ready to go to their big brother's funeral. It was a beautiful funeral service. When something tragic happens, you see who really comes to your rescue. All our loved ones from our past and present came to support us and show their love.

Sadie was heartbroken as was I. All the siblings and immediate family members were heartbroken. There was so much confusion. I remember asking God, why would you do this? Why would you break her heart like you broke mine when I was a little boy? Why would you do this to me again? I have dealt with the pain of my father's choices all my life—thoughts of wanting to take my own life, fear, and pain. I pleaded to God, why am I reliving this hell again?

My self-esteem took a big hit; I blamed myself as I had done my whole life. Why did I not see this coming? I am a failure! I am a failure of a stepfather! I am a failure as a husband. It should have been me! I was having thoughts of ending my life.

12

MORE SURPRISE PARTIES

Sadie is an amazing woman and friend. She battled through a hell only very few have ever gone through. She faced darkness and found the light. She is an astonishing mother that took a horrific sadness and came out the other side. I thank her for teaching me love and helping me to be a better person.

My wife was going through complete and total despair. For years after this tragic time, she struggled mentality and physically. Her body started to break down from the mental trauma. I would try to massage her body for hours to relieve her pain, praying in my heart for God to heal her. There was a lot of self-isolation. She worked a little and took a lot of time off the following year. I remained working, but pretty much everything in our lives had fallen apart. We did have some spiritual moments through that time after her son's passing. These were moments that could only be explained as divine rather than simply coincidence. These were signs to remind us we had divine help looking over us, that everything was going to be ok even if everything did not feel or seem ok. We put the children into therapy. My wife and I were also going to therapy and a support group. It was just complete and total turmoil for months and even years after his passing. I was absolutely dying inside watching my wife literally falling apart mentally and physically. I cried millions of tears over her pain, praying for hours on end for God to heal her.

This was another time in my life when the surprise party thoughts came up constantly. I dreamed of the surprise party all the time. I really visualized it, seeing, and knowing it was going to happen. What we were going through seemed so surreal; I saw me and my wife coming home to a big surprise party of everyone standing there and saying, Surprise, it has not been real! It was all just a test to see how you did. These thoughts were just like the ones I had throughout my life of my father, only now the party's size was much bigger. I remember having many suicidal thoughts; they would not stop playing out in my mind all the time. They were so unsettling and repetitive; I would try to tell myself I could not possibly follow through with it and I especially did not want to add to the pain my partner was already dealing with. I was fighting the voices in my head. It was just a complete and total chaos of emotions!

I have never lost anyone to a car wreck or any other accident, only to old age or suicide. This is all I have ever known. I have even had many friends and other family members besides my father and my wife's son pass away due to suicide. For some reason, suicide has gravitated toward me my entire life. I also have numerous people close to me who have also lost their family members to suicide. It is a hellish turmoil that has followed me all my life.

13

REMEMBERING DÉJÀ VU

My partner called me at work one day about a year after her son's passing. The first words out of her mouth were, do you remember our déjà vu and where we were? I thought back to the déjà vu that occurred before we were married. She and I had talked about it over the years and it was kind of a meaningful, special thing to us. Instantly, it meant even more; the occurrence finally made some sense! On the day, her son died, our phones started ringing at the same spot where our déjà vu started when we were getting off the freeway that day. We had pulled over in a little driveway to a small cemetery, the same spot where we turned the car around to go to the hospital.

I do not know if there is any meaning to this, and you can call it coincidence or whatever you like, but my wife and I knew that this was a message from God telling us that he was watching out for us. I do not know what the meaning of it all was, but at least it gave us a little bit of peace.

14

BREATHING

About a year after the death of my partner's son, there was a big separation between her and myself. We grew apart from each other. She moved out and we lived in separate places, raising our families separately. We stayed married however, and we would talk on and off. This went on for a few years.

During these years of separation, I learned a lot about myself. I did a lot of studying and learning about self-help and manifestation. I studied the eastern philosophies and listened to a lot of inspirational speakers. I did a lot of letting go of my programming from the beliefs that were ingrained in me by my ancestors. I tried meditation and being in the present moment. Meditation and being in the present moment were both a struggle and did not work too well for me at that time in my life. There was a lot of chaos in my life and mind. I was doing a lot of soul-searching and praying, really working to find peace. I was not doing so well. At this time in my life was when I started to learn the second discovery insight of breathing and the third discovery insight of being present.

To enjoy good health, to bring true happiness to one's family, to bring peace to all, one must first discipline and control one's own mind. If a man can control his mind, he can find the way to enlightenment, and all wisdom and virtue will naturally come to him." -Siddhartha Gautama

Now that I have given you a small look into my life, you can see that I have been down a lot of different paths on my life journey. Despite the many trials and hardships that I have faced, I would not change one thing about my life; I am thankful for all my experiences. I am a blessed man to have experienced all these beautiful, life-changing experiences and to come out even stronger, happier, and wiser. It is my hope that as you face your trials, you can implement these discovery insights into your life as I have learned to. I did not implement these discovery insights until later in my life, but I know if I would have known the benefits of them when I was younger, my life would have been much more peaceful and rewarding. These insights have brought my life pure bliss, happiness, and the means to a healthy and wealthy life.

    I encourage you to open your mind, step outside your comfort zone, turn off your old programming, and trust that there is more out there for you to learn that will help you grow. I promise you there is more out there, more than you can even begin to fathom. The power these insights hold is endless and there is no limit to what you can do with them if you implement them into your life. I encourage you to investigate and study them more thoroughly on your own.

THE SURPRISE PARTY

The second discovery insight of breathing is a seemingly easy thing that requires a fair bit of work to see results from. There is a spiritual side to this insight, one that is powerful and meaningful. What is the very first thing you did when you came into this beautiful world? What is the very last thing you will do when you leave this world? The answer is breathing. Breathing is one of the most divine, beautiful actions we perform every second of every day. Breathing is a bodily phenomenon that our bodies do unwittingly, yet we can also learn to control it. Breathing is heavenly and divine. Your breathing helps regulate your nervous system.

It is best to simply start by practicing taking deep breaths. Inhale deeply through your nose and exhale through your mouth. Let the exhale go all the way out, pushing it deep from the bottom of your stomach. Open your throat, airway, and mouth wide. Then take a deep breath, inhaling big enough to see your abdomen move outward. As you exhale, push all the air out until you see your abdomen move inward. As you are exhaling, you will start to feel your heartbeat and your exhaling breath take rhythm and connect together. This is the rhythm you want to take place. As you transition at the top of your breath when inhaling and at the bottom of your breath when exhaling, try to make this a continuous flow, never stopping completely or for too long. Eventually this practice will come naturally.

Another breathing practice to try is forcing a deep, hard inhale and then forcing the exhale out just as deep and hard. It so refreshing. Try to remember to practice these simple deep breaths when you are afraid or feeling angry.

I first started practicing these breathing techniques at one of the most stressful times in my life; I was trying anything

I could to find peace. I would find myself holding my breath for such long amounts of time, I would literally have to force myself to breathe. I was so stressed, grinding my teeth in frustration, and holding my breath for half a minute or longer. At first, I started to focus on my breathing and how long I was holding my breath. I was surprised at how long I was holding my breath. As easy as breathing should be, it was very difficult for me at first; I had held it for so long throughout my lifetime. My poor breathing was driven by a lifetime of stress.

I encourage you to practice this insight over and over throughout the day, every day. Practice it before you go to sleep, as you are lying down, or when you are falling asleep. Practice it when you wake up. Practice it when you are driving—you will find it calming. Practice it while at work. Eventually, you will determine when the best times are for you to practice.

After learning this simple breathing pattern, breathing this way throughout the day, and eventually mastering this simple deep-breathing pattern, I encourage you to learn another breathing technique for relaxation. This breathing pattern is called the "4-7-8" pattern. It promotes deeper sleep, releases stress, and calms the nervous system. You simply inhale through your nose for four seconds, filling your lungs and your head full of oxygen, hold it in your lungs for seven seconds, then slowly exhale through your mouth for eight seconds, exhaling all the air out, all the way from deep in your stomach.

There are many benefits to these breathing techniques. Your inhaling breath is a new sensation of love and energy that you are feeding your beautiful new soul. As you exhale, you are letting go of all your old energy. Remind yourself how perfect and beautiful you are while you are practicing this new insight.

I want to add a quick note about my breathing, a problem you might also have. I have had my nose broken numerous times in my life from sports thus restricting my air intake during the relaxation breathing pattern. I was not getting enough air on my inhale during the four-second step and thus had to change up my breathing pattern to better suit my needs. I had to do a longer inhale both through my nose and mouth to allow more air to come in. You can do all your inhaling through your mouth if needed, though this tends to dry out your mouth which can sometimes be uncomfortable. You always want to exhale out through your mouth because you can get a much larger volume of air out—this is key to these breathing exercises. It is ok to change up your breathing techniques in any way that suits your needs. What is most important is that you are learning and practicing this insight daily.

I promise if you start to do this you will feel a new peace. You will feel a new energy within. Your body might take time to adapt to this new breathing pattern, but it is rewarding and so refreshing. You will feel and be healthier.

Please teach these breathing exercises to your children, family, and friends. I used to practice breathing with my children when we went skiing while we were on the chairlift. Doing this while we were up in the cold, clean, crisp mountain air was heavenly. It cleaned our souls with pure mountain air.

There are many immensely powerful breathing patterns and techniques out there to study and learn. Please investigate and find them, implement them, study them, and practice them daily. There are methods that can make you stronger and healthier, even techniques that have been proven to take away pain such as those taught to pregnant mothers in anticipation of childbirth.

I encourage you to make daily breathing exercises a goal and write it down. When working on these breathing patterns, try to do it for a continuous three minutes, working your way up to five minutes, and then to ten. Make your goal longer and longer. As you are breathing, continue to focus the whole time on keeping your mind completely calm.

Please remember to practice your breathing when you are stressed. Remember to tell yourself how perfect and beautiful you are while you practice this insight. Breathe love into that beautiful soul of yours, feed your soul, and let your love flow.

15

Be Present

The next insight I started to implement during this time in my life was the third discovery insight of being present. This was a hard insight for me to learn, but once I did, it was both rewarding and powerful.

I am sure some of you have heard about staying in the present moment from eastern philosophies or religious practices. I can tell you that staying in the present moment is not a religious teaching; it is a tremendously healthy way of being good to yourself.

During the years after my partner lost her son and we separated, I learned a lot of beautiful life lessons and many hard ones as well. I was really struggling inside. Everything around me was falling apart. I started to listen to some fantastic and inspiring motivational speakers. I was praying and trying everything I could do to possibly get us and life to work out again. I was doing breathing work, meditating, and listening to the motivational speakers; it was at that time in my life that I was introduced to being in the present moment.

I had studied and learned about this concept over the years and I could never figure it out. What was the purpose of staying in the present moment? Why would I want to *be* in the present moment? Why would I want to *stay* in the present moment? At that time in my life, the present was the last place I wanted to be! From what I had researched, it seemed to be a far-reaching teaching throughout time and primarily practiced in eastern philosophy. I researched and investigated it but was still confused on what staying in the present moment truly looked like.

From my studies I learned that the future is not real—the future is anticipation. The past is only a memory, there is nothing that can become of the past. The only real thing is the present moment. I was still confused. One day after this troubled time, it came to me. Staying present was hard to do, but it was a life-changing lesson to learn. I cannot tell you how valuable it is. If I would have known this simple change of mindset throughout all my years of having a mind full of racing thoughts, I can absolutely promise you I would look and feel younger. If I could have learned to stop those thoughts or even just slow them down and stay in the present moment, things might have been different. I went through so many hard times, fighting all my demons inside, and if I had just known how to stay present, I would have been able to stay calm and be at peace. I would have stayed young and grown young. I would have been a completely different person than I am today.

Your racing mind is killing you in more ways than you could ever imagine. Your negative thoughts and the energy you put into them are slowly killing you. Negative thoughts will diminish your health and wellness. Be young, grow young, live a peaceful life. Practice stopping your racing mind and start living in the present moment. Let go of the overthinking and worrying and embrace being present.

THE SURPRISE PARTY

When I first started practicing staying in the present moment, I could literally only do it for about three seconds at the most. My mind was so chaotic and distressed from years of mental abuse, it took all I had to stop it for that short amount of time.

You do not need to be sitting on a mat and meditating to be in the present moment, as I'm sure many of you have seen in the media or on TV. Staying present doesn't mean sitting cross-legged with arms placed on your knees, eyes closed; being present can take whatever relaxing form is available and easy for you. One of my yoga instructors made me realize that it is not about sitting in the typical meditation-yoga position—which is uncomfortable to some—but rather about being comfortable and relaxed. Relax—life is so busy and stressful. Relax and take care of yourself and practice staying in the present moment. Do this anywhere you can and get as comfortable as you possibly can. You can do this when you are falling asleep at night—simply be still. You can do this almost anywhere, though I would recommend that when first learning this, it is best to find a quiet place. Once you have mastered this insight, then you will be able to block everything out and stay in the moment while in the most chaotic of places. I have yet to master this, but I will. I learned to do this at night when I could not sleep from the stress in my life. It is so peaceful to shut your thoughts off and let your mind be at rest.

This is a life-changing practice, one we should all strive to practice every day of our lives. I encourage you to practice this while at work, just relaxing, and on the couch, or one of my favorite places to practice is outside after a hike while watching the sunset.

There are three parts to each of us: the mind, the heart, and the soul, which together form the trinity. Your mind does all your thinking, running wild all day long with your thoughts. Your heart leads you with your emotions. And finally, your soul is the heavenly side of your earthly body. Your soul lives within your body and is the part of heaven that is here on earth. I encourage you to learn to let all three work together as one. While you are practicing staying present, let your soul be the leader of your heart and mind. Your soul will direct your mind to relax and let your heart know it is at peace. Make an agreement with your mind, heart and soul and will your soul to be the divine commander when practicing being present. Trust the wisdom of your soul to know what is best and what is safe. Your soul will put you where you belong.

To begin the practice of being in the present moment, first start with the simple breathing exercises I explained in the second discovery insight. I recommend as you are learning this insight to stay with the basic breathing pattern. I find it best to start your breathing for about three to five minutes to calm down and get comfortable. Your breathing aligns the body and gets the body and mind in rhythm. As you are breathing, close your eyes and look at the back of your eyelids. Just investigate the darkness of the back of your eyelids. To start, slowly calm your mind down. You can start by maybe thanking your higher being or the universe. You can try to think of beautiful places or calming, happy times in your life. Slow your worrying thoughts down into calming thoughts. As you are breathing and looking at the back of your eyelids, stop all thought and look into the darkness. Connect your mind with your breathing.

Let your eyes and eyelids relax, becoming completely at peace. Sometimes you will see complete darkness or sometimes you might even see stars. You could possibly even see images in the darkness. While you are doing this, start your relaxation breathing, keeping it going the entire time. Your breathing will start to come naturally, blocking all thoughts out. This is when beautiful, spiritual things can happen. Always pay attention to your breathing—it is valuable for your peace. If you fall asleep, that is fine. Calmly wake yourself up and keep focusing on peace and staying in the present moment.

This next part is especially important. As you are working on being present and peaceful, stop all your thoughts. No more doubts, fears, or negativity, only peace and relaxation. Let go of all thoughts. Stop your mind from racing and just relax and breathe. Remind yourself that what you see is the only thing that is real. All your thoughts trying to race into your mind are not real; they do not exist. Do this for some time. Just stare into the darkness at the back of your eyelids.

You will find your mind drifting to thoughts of everything from work to disagreements with people to what you are going to buy at the store. You will find your mind plays out all different versions of the past and the possible future. While you are looking at the back of your eyelids, stop these stories from playing out in your mind. These stories are not real; you cannot predict the future or relive the past. You will be absolutely astonished at how busy your mind is. Don't get frustrated and do not worry or feel guilty if your mind wanders; stay positive and just bring it back to your breathing and the peace of not thinking.

As I said, I really struggled with this at first while practicing it. Sometimes my mind was in such a chaotic state—my "monkey mind" as it is often referred to by practitioners of staying in the present—that I had to stop and say aloud to myself, "Stop all thinking and relax," which would tell my soul this it was in control of what I was thinking. If it is helpful, you can calm your mind by praying, but only pray by giving thanks.

You can practice being present all day, every day. At the beginning, it's easiest to practice this with your eyes closed, but once you have become a master at it, you can do it with your eyes open and then there is nowhere that you can't be present and mindful. I practice it with my eyes open simply while I am driving. As I'm driving, I look straight ahead to the vehicle in front of me, stopping my mind from wandering and blocking any incoming thoughts. I tell myself, *the only thing that is real is right here, right now.* I also practice while at the gym working out, while at work on my lunch break, or even on the beach looking at the sunrise or sunset.

Being present is a powerful insight. I want to warn you as you start to get good at this insight that you might begin to experience some spiritual events—don't be alarmed! You might experience episodes of pleasant tingling within your body or a peaceful buzzing within. Relax and know you are experiencing a new enlightenment from your new spiritual insight. This is only an introduction into this powerful, spiritual, ancient practice. Trust yourself, trust the process, and trust the insight. And have peaceful, spiritual fun with it.

At times in your life when you feel like you are losing your mind—after a divorce, the loss of a loved one, or work stresses—is when being in the present moment is most vital to calming your mind and being at peace. There have been times in my life when I felt like I was absolutely going out of my mind with thoughts of the past and present. I look back now and wish I had known how to use this power during those difficult times in my life. When you start to understand how to be present, you'll see how relaxing it is, like finally getting to take a break from a race you've been running for years. Your mind will just fall into a relaxing, tranquil state; it feels like your mind is finally at home. Stop the mental race we are all running throughout our daily lives and find the peace and calm in the present moment.

I have read books and listed to teachings on this practice that claim that ten minutes of meditation is equivalent to about 30 minutes of sleep. I can vouch for how effective meditation and being present are for relaxing.

Being in the present moment can be a part of any religious practice you may already have. It can be implemented into a religious, spiritual, or agnostic lifestyle. Add the insight before or after prayer. This insight is a peaceful way of being still and enhancing your religious beliefs.

Please study this and learn it—make it a goal and know it. Once you know it, I encourage you to teach it to your children, family, and friends. Your loved ones, both young and old, will stay young. Encourage them to learn and implement this insight and practice it throughout their lives. Teach them to stop and practice it before a school test, sporting event, or any stressful moment they may face. They will succeed with ease throughout their busy lives.

Remember to always tell yourself how perfect you are and how beautiful you are while you are practicing this insight.

During those years I pretty much spent all my time working. When I was not at work, I was praying and exercising to find peace. It was a stressful time. I was alone and basically had nothing to do. My boys were getting older and hanging out with friends more. I remember getting in my car and my day consisting of going to work, exercising, meditating, and praying. My weekends consisted of getting up, going for a drive, and then going and meditating to find some peace. I would then go to the gym and work out for quite a long time, probably four-plus hours. This became a routine, but it was very peaceful. I remember thinking that this was all I wanted to do and all I wanted in life. All I want is just peace and love; I don't need material possessions in my life. I loved my little vehicle which was enough to haul me and my four boys around. I was happy with my simple lifestyle and thought I would be a Buddhist monk if I could. There are Buddhist monks that live in monasteries in Tibet, India, Thailand, etc. who just pray and meditate all day long. These Buddhist monks' lives consist of waking up and meditating for hours, eating, showing love, and taking care of their small daily needs. They are usually sponsored by someone within their spiritual community for any monetary needs they might have. Their lives consist entirely of living a beautiful, peaceful life of mediation. They require truly little to live on; their food and other sustenance is grown on their own. These beautiful souls are sponsored to meditate for good, love, and peace for of all mankind. I dreamed of living their lifestyle.

16

TRIATHLON

It had now been six years since the passing of my wife's son and things had gotten quite overwhelming between myself and my partner. We just lived completely separate lives. Sadie and her children were living in a little condo up the road from where I lived with my boys. We were friends on and off over the years. One day Sadie told me that she had to move out of her place since her landlord was selling the condo, she lived in. We did a lot of talking and decided maybe it was time that we try again and move in together. We decided to buy a home together and started looking at houses. After a short time looking, I decided that I could build us a home. Between myself and my partner, we did just that. We worked hard and started the process. It was all a lot of work: we had gotten back together, gotten the loan process done, and started to build the home.

Years earlier when I had quit drinking, I had purchased a mountain bike. I started riding the bike and that evolved into many more hobbies: road biking, boxing, running, swimming, skiing, and weightlifting. I also competed in most of these sports. I exercised a lot throughout those years. I also started competing in triathlons. It was a lot of fun. I even won some of the triathlon events in my division! Basically, my alcohol addiction had turned into an exercising addiction. This seems to happen to a lot of people with addictions; they trade the unhealthy addiction for a healthier one. My exercising sessions would go on for hours and hours. I had gotten big into triathlons and become so passionate about them. I loved competing in them. It was such an outlet for me from all the commotion of everything and the sadness that was at home and within. When you are on a bike ride for over 100 miles, swimming for miles, and running for hours on end, you have lots of time to think and pray. My mind would race and ponder over all that had gone on in my life. Many times, I cried during these events, even filling my swim googles with tears of heartbreak. The destructive voices got to be a lot, but I forged on. While training for all those hours and miles, I prayed and prayed and thought and thought. This went on for years. I had done half-triathlons and a lot of smaller distance Olympic- and sprint-sized triathlons but decided to do my first full-distance triathlon. To participate in one of these full events takes a lot of training and a lot of money. I was training for eight to ten hours a day. The expense of one of these events was a lot. By the time you get to the race in another state and pay the race fees and all the other small costs like food, lodging, and vehicle expenses, you will have spent thousands of dollars.

After going through the home loan process, my partner and I had closed on the home loan and were ready to start building our home the day after I got home from my full triathlon in Lake Tahoe. It was an exciting time for my partner and me—we were building this new home, which was also a big fear for me. The last time I had built homes was when I was general contracting when the economy crashed in 2008, and

THE SURPRISE PARTY

I lost everything. So, going out on a limb and starting construction on a new home was a big fear for me. What if I can't get a contractor there? What if the economy falls again as I am building the home? I knew I could do it, but a lot of fears resurfaced along with self-doubt.

We went to Lake Tahoe, Nevada to participate in the triathlon. It was so beautiful! I absolutely love Lake Tahoe. There is a piece of my soul that lives there with its glorious beauty. We arrived the day before the race started and drove around, scoping out the race route. After a nice, carb-filled supper, I slept uncommonly well for the night before a race. My sleep is usually disturbed by race jitters. I got up early the next morning and headed to the race entrance, excited to be doing my first full triathlon.

The race started with a bang. I completed the first leg of the triathlon (a 2.4-mile swim) with great time and feeling good. For a 265-pound guy carrying a lot of weight over a lot of miles, I was doing quite well. I was loving it! The next leg was a 112-mile bike ride through the stunning mountains of Lake Tahoe. I got dressed and climbed onto my bike. My bike times were going great; I was about 96 miles into my ride when I approached an intersection. As I approached, I could see police officers stopping vehicles to let the bikers go through. As there was a bigger gap between bike riders, the police officers would allow vehicles to go through the intersection. As I approached the intersection, there was a gap between me and the next rider ahead of myself. The police officers allowed a car to go through between us. When the car went through, I was just about into the intersection. Just then, the car following the first car thought they were to follow. The second car came into the intersection and collided with me, ejecting me off my bike and up over the hood. I went crashing on the other side of the car and landed on the road.

My adrenaline immediately kicked in! I lay there for a minute and told the police officer to just let me breathe and get reoriented. I told the officer I was going to finish the race. After putting in all those hours of training and all that money, nothing was going to stop me from finishing the race. The police officer disagreed, telling me that I was done with the race and the only way I was going anywhere was in an ambulance. He then said, "And sir, your bike is definitely not going anywhere." The bike was too damaged. I lay there on the road with tears in my eyes—tears of disappointment and tears of terrible pain. My back felt like it was on fire, like there were hot needles going into my spine.

The ambulance arrived and took me to the nearest hospital. As I arrived at the hospital, the nurse said she needed my information to call an emergency contact. I let her know that I would prefer to call my wife myself. The last time the hospital had called her had been to tell her about her son and I knew I could not let her experience that again. The nurse gave me the phone and I called her. I told her I was ok, but I was not doing so well. I let her know my back was in an extreme amount of pain. She said she was on her way to come and get me. The medical staff took x-rays and gave me injections to try to subside the pain. Finally, after quite a few injections, my pain was manageable, and the hospital sent me on my way and told me to follow up with a doctor.

At that time, I believed that I was going to go home to heal and get better. And then once I was healthy, I was going to get back to training and do another full triathlon. I believed nothing was going to slow me down. I wanted to redeem myself and compete once again. I also knew that as soon we arrived home, I was going to start building a home. I was now beaten up quite badly, but I felt with a few weeks' time, I would recover. I was planning to do a lot of the work building the home. My partner and I arrived home after a long and painful ten-hour drive.

I felt like a failure. Even though I knew not finishing the race was out of my control, I felt like pretty much everything I had ever done was wrong. I beat myself up over not finishing that race. After a week, I still had horrific pain in my lower back. We started building the home and I did my best to help, but I was in so much pain. I went to see my doctor after a week to see why the pain had not let up. He sent me for an MRI which showed ruptures and tears in my discs that were quite bad. Between my wife and the little I could do as well as the help of other family members, we went forward building the home. I could not lift a thing; all the lifting had to be done by my wife and others. I was in appallingly uncomfortable pain. I remember lying there on the basement floor, the cold concrete on my back, trying to get some relief and crying in pain. But eventually we got the home built.

17

MANIFESTATION

My wife and I moved into our new home together. Life was about the same as when we had last lived together; Sadie was struggling with life and I was not doing well now with the pain in my lower back. Not too long after living together, I once again decided to move out. I was in so much pain trying to survive, and this was adding to our relationship stress.

One day I went to the gym to swim, one of the only activities I could still do that was low impact on my back. I did a lot of swimming after my injury and I still do to this day. As I started to get out of my car at the gym, I fell to the ground from hip and leg pain. I could hardly walk. The pain was unbearable. I somehow hobbled and got back into my vehicle and went home and tried to lie down. After a few hours of not getting any relief, I went to see my physical therapist and he worked with me, but nothing seemed to help. I then went to see my chiropractor who also did not help. Finally, I went to my family doctor to get some relief and he was unable to help me. I went to three doctors in one day. The pain was so unreal. It was odd pain for me because it was not my back so much as my leg and hip; I could not move them. I thought my hip and thighbone were broken for some reason. I broke my thighbone in three places when I was a child, so I know what that pain feels like. I could hardly walk. That night I was in so much pain I drove myself to the emergency room.

    I arrived at the hospital emergency room and spoke with the doctor, letting him know that I did not know what happened, but my thighbone and hip were broken. I thought maybe my hip bone somehow crumbled from the triathlon accident where the ball joint connected to the thighbone. I knew, without a doubt, that they were broken. After speaking to the doctor, he said, "I am confident that your thighbone and hip are not broken." He went on to say that he was confident it was my back causing the pain. He explained that the nerves had been pinched by the discs and asked me to do another MRI to prove it. "I promise you, if it's not your back, then yes, we will x-ray your hip to see if it is broken." I agreed and they wheeled me in for the MRI and, of course, the doctor was correct; my discs had finally crumbled from the impact of the bike accident. Once discs are as irreparably damaged as mine, they start to break down and fall apart over time. Once this occurs, the pieces of the broken disc can lodge against the spinal cord, pinching and damaging the nerves. These nerves being pinched off was causing my leg and hip to feel broken and not able to move. The doctor explained that they were going to have to do an emergency surgery—a discectomy—on my back to retrieve the broken discs that had been pressing against my spinal cord. I was so blessed to get the best neurosurgeon there is for my surgery; he just happened to be on-call that night. My doctor is an astonishing person for his ability to do the things that he does. I will be forever grateful for his knowledge and blessed,

THE SURPRISE PARTY

skilled hands. All my doctors and medical staff I have been blessed with over the years that have helped me with my back pain have been a godsend to me. I am blessed, I thank them all! The doctor removed all the pieces of the discs and I left the hospital after a few days. I went home feeling sore, but much better because I could walk slowly with limitations. My doctor ordered me to only do light walking, no bending, and physical therapy.

After about a month since my surgery, I was doing well and went into the kitchen to put a dish into the top of the dishwasher, just turning to the side and not bending. The next thing I knew, I had fallen to my knees and again was in total pain, feeling the same as I had before my surgery. I had total numbness in my leg and thighbone, and it felt again as though my hip was broken. I went back to the emergency room feeling the same pain as my first trip.

I spoke with the doctor and he explained to me they were going to have to go in again and this time do a fusion in my back. I was really against back surgery, but when they tell you it is an emergency, I guess you have no choice. And the pain was excruciating; surgery was essential. They scheduled the surgery. The doctor ended up fusing two of my discs. A third disc was also quite damaged, but the doctor decided that it was probably going to be ok and to let it stay. To perform a back fusion, the doctor opens your back up and goes into your spinal column and removes the old, damaged discs. The doctor then installs metal rods into your back to support your vertebrae in place of the missing discs. I have metal rods in my back to this day. It is still quite painful, but I try to live life to the fullest. It has slowed me down though. I lived for four years with this horrific pain and contemplated taking my life many times because of it; the pain made me angry and want to give up. But I am so fortunate that I can walk and that I can move. My injuries could have been much worse. I try to stay active and I do a lot of swimming, walking, and hiking. I just try take care of myself to keep the pain down. I am truly the most blessed guy ever!

A few years after my accident and surgeries, I was urged to listen to a motivational speaker by a friend. Without much information, I listened to this speaker one day and was inspired by this beautiful soul. I started listening to his podcast and learning about his life story and started to laugh out loud the further I got: his story was almost identical to mine! He too was on the bike ride portion of a triathlon and was struck by a car. His injuries were a lot more severe than mine; his vertebrae were crushed and severed which left him paralyzed. His story is beautiful. I do not want to say his name due to legal reasons; however, I encourage you to look him up by searching, "How I healed myself after breaking six vertebrae." I do not want to go too much into his story, but please look him up and listen to him. He has many life-changing, motivational speeches. I wish I would have known his teachings soon after my accident. I possibly would have had a different outcome, learning from his faith.

It was at this time in my life when I started to find the fourth and final discovery insight of manifesting. The discovery insight is manifesting all your needs, wants, dreams, and desires. Manifesting is all done by love. Manifestation has been practiced for hundreds of years, all the way back to ancient times, using the connection between your mind, body, and soul, then adding God and the universe. The combination of all these magnificent powers is the most powerful healing and willing tool there ever was. Manifesting is understanding that everything in your life happens for you, not to you.

Manifesting is thinking of a desire, want, or need and then sending it out to God and the universe. By doing this, your desire, want, or need will be delivered to you. You can even manifest your body to grow young instead of old. We are always focused on getting old. Change that thought process to manifest your body to grow young. Do not even let a single thought of growing old enter your mind. It is never too late to manifest growing young. Put all your hopes and dreams into your manifestations to obtain them. Manifesting is real and powerful.

You can manifest to the universe or you can manifest to God or both. God and the universe are your partners in manifesting. All three of you together form one team in manifestation. God and the universe want you to have all your desires and dreams.

There are three rules when manifesting. A lot of people forget these three rules and then find that their efforts don't work in their favor. Trust me, it works if done correctly!

First rule: you cannot manifest something that affects another human being's free will. For example, asking the universe for a friend to change his or her mind to fall in love with you. This will not work in manifesting. God, the universe, and you cannot change another human being's free will. No one can make your friend change their mind to fall in love with you. This only applies to personal free will; business free will, on the other hand, is different. Business free will may look like manifesting for your supervisor to change his or her mind to reevaluate your pay and give you a promotion or maybe manifesting for your colleagues to be nicer and kinder to you at work. These are business-related free will manifestations. Remember: you cannot ask for personal free will with your manifestation, but you can ask for business free will manifestations.

The second rule adds to the second discovery insight of being present. I coached you that being in the present means recognizing that the thoughts in your mind do not exist and that you cannot predict the future or relive the past. In actuality, there is one type of forthcoming thought that *is* real while being present: these are your manifestations. I have found that while being in the present moment is one of the best times to practice manifesting. For instance, when I can stop during the day to practice being in the present moment for roughly 15 minutes, I find it a good time for the last three to five minutes to take time and manifest. Your manifesting thoughts while staying in the present moment are the only thoughts that are real. And yes, those manifestation thoughts are real, and they do come true.

The third rule: there is plenty to go around, but you need to be respectful to God and to the universe. You cannot be careless or wasteful of your manifestation. For example, if you manifest for the money to pay your power bill and your manifestation comes true, you can't squander the money instead of paying the power bill—it does not matter that there is plenty. You cannot be wasteful! God and the universe will only respond to love and good, not carelessness. Please remember these three rules when manifesting; they are absolute lawful when it comes to manifesting.

THE SURPRISE PARTY

I believed for many years that the only way to get something was the hard way. I also told myself when something went well or things were going right in my life that bad times were on their way. This way of believing and thinking is completely wrong and is a programmed pattern. There is plenty and there is no sacrifice you must make for good to happen in your life. You are worthy and deserving of everything you want. I had to work hard to change my mindset; to this day I still need to work on it at times. Remember, God and the universe are your partners in life and in manifesting. You can manifest to any God that you believe in or manifest to a higher being. You then send your manifestation out to the universe. If you are agnostic, that is beautiful! Just manifest to the universe.

The more people to help you in your manifestation, the better the outcome. When manifesting to the universe, you are mentally bringing everyone in through your energy to help you in your desires. For example, if you are looking to purchase that perfect home, while manifesting to the universe you might mentally call in the perfect people to help you in your quest: the lender, the underwriter, the seller selling the home to put it up for sale at the perfect time. All the timing and everyone involved will come together for that one perfect home.

If it is a manifestation that you can work on with a spouse, partner, or someone close, by working on it together you will be astonished at how much better the outcome will be. The more involved, the more spiritual the outcome for your manifestation. Two minds are more powerful than one. If all human beings in the world would manifest together, we could stop world hunger. I could write a whole second book on this topic alone.

Try to comprehend the power of all human beings manifesting together for love and peace in the world. There would only be love and peace and no world hunger in our beautiful world.

Everyone has manifested in his or her life to some degree, you just may not have realized it. Most everyone has wanted something and worked for it. You thought of the want or need, worked toward it, and it came true. For instance, a child wants a bike. The child thinks about it all the time, daydreaming while sitting in school and thinking of it while he or she drifts off to sleep, then dreaming about it. The bike then comes to the child eventually. Yes, the child worked for it and maybe earned money for it, but the bike came to the child. The money came in place for the child to purchase the bike. This is manifesting. This could even be something small like thinking of an old friend and then seeing that friend the next day. This is manifesting. If you look back on your life, you will see many of these instances of manifestation. You might not believe in manifestation and tell yourself that you earned the money for the item you received. Yes, you might have earned it, however, it was money that you did not plan on and it came to you. I will tell you this: as you get better with manifesting, it does become easier. You will then believe it and see it come to you.

Manifesting can also work against you. Since manifesting is pure thought, fixating on something bad can manifest that bad thing happening to you. For example, if you are worried about getting a flat tire on a long drive, stressing and worrying over it incessantly, you are manifesting the tire to go flat. Try changing your worry and stress into something good and asking the universe and God to arrive home safe and sound with no issues from the long drive. Shoot, you might as well add to your manifesting and ask for a set of four new tires for your vehicle. Try it and watch your manifestation succeed!

To begin manifesting, first decide what you want. Be extremely specific when manifesting. Have a clear understanding of what you want. Remember you are worthy of all your desires. I would suggest starting small like manifesting getting the parking spot closest to the store entrance, money to pay your power bill, or getting a new TV. Start with small manifestations and then it can grow from there as you believe and start to see it work.

Once you have decided what you want, it is best to write it down and treat it like you would a goal. Be extremely specific; if, say, it is a money manifestation write down the exact dollar amount. Write down your money needs and write down how your desire is going to help you. What is it going to do in your favor? For instance, the bike you want will help you get to work rather than driving your car that causes pollution. And the bike will save money on gas. The bike is going to give you needed exercise. Your new bike is going to be fun to ride across the scenic mountainside.

Next, see it in your mind. See the bike and you riding it and enjoying it. Daydream about it like you did when you were a child in school. Dream about it and see it like you did your junior high school crush who was so cute that you wanted to go to the dance with. You dreamed of kissing him or her. You saw the two of you dancing at the school dance to your favorite songs. We have all done this type of daydreaming at some point in our lives. This is the type of thinking you need to put into your manifestation.

Next, believe in it and see it as if it is already taken place. If you are seeing it and believing it, say it out loud, feel it, smell it. You see and know you already have it and you enjoy it. You have got to say it as if it has already occurred or is already in your hands.

Finally, it will come to you. Have fun with the bike. Love it, enjoy it, take care of it, and be thankful for it.

It is not your concern how your manifestation will take place. Don't overthink it. It is God's and the universe's choice; allow them to do it for you. Do not have any worries on how it will happen. Your job is to be absolutely clear on your manifestation. Just sit back and relax and know the work will be done.

Manifesting is often only viewed as asking for something materialistic or monetary. This is not the case; you can manifest almost anything if it is manifested with love. You can manifest for health reasons, education, or even personal help. You can heal your physical body through manifestation. You can even heal the physical pain of others. Simply manifest to heal your body and your mind to heal your pain. You can do the same practice to fix and heal others! Yes, you can heal the pain of others through your manifestation. I have personally done this to another human being in my life.

After all the work I had done to rid my mental and physical pain in my life, I was finally able to manifest it all out of my life. I manifested the pain to all be gone and for me to be completely done with it. I manifested to no longer have thoughts of sadness and pain. I manifested for my horrific physical pain from my bicycle accident to be gone and sent out of my life to the universe.

THE SURPRISE PARTY

I needed to start letting go of the pain and trauma endured to my body from my triathlon accident. I started in on the discovery insights to finally be done and fix my body as a whole. I did all the manifestation steps to fix my body and take away the pain. I willed it all to be done and gone. I have healed my pain from my triathlon accident. I did not know the powers behind manifestation until after my surgeries or else I would have used manifestation before them. It was not until after my surgeries that I started to really practice manifesting. Yes, I received surgery, but even after the surgery I was destined to live with pain all my life. I have since manifested and healed my injuries to the point where I can enjoy myself now and be free of pain.

Just as I have done, you too can heal pain in yourself and others through the practice of manifestation. Any pain and suffering you may experience, whether it be arthritis, an injury, or a body abnormality like cancer, heart disease or failed kidneys, can be manifested away. Mental trauma such as depression and bipolar disorder can be manifested away. You can heal yourself by practicing these insights. Manifest it and will it out of your life! Thank the trauma for protecting you from a much worse trauma. Then send it off with love. You can do this! Take care of your body, love it, and heal it.

Healing the body through manifestation is as easy as thinking of yourself or someone else. Think of the damaged part of the body. Imagine you are looking at it on the inside of the body, looking at the different cells that come together to create the tissue and organs and then seeing all the body phenomena working together to heal the damaged body part. See all the moving parts of the injured organ. See the lifeblood and oxygen moving to heal that broken or damaged body part. Picture loving and nurturing it from your soul and then sending it love to heal it. Visualize it coming back to life and turning a healthy color. See the healthy new organ and body part come alive. Manifest moving the cells to form healthy tissue to bring it back to life. Then see your brain firing the transponders to fix the nervous system to heal the damaged body part. See the lungs sending beautiful, clean, healing oxygen to all your organs. See the ventricular system healing your beautiful, young, healthy body. The cerebrospinal fluid is moving and bringing the damaged body part to a healing state of repairs. See your nervous system rewiring your brain and billions of nerve cells to the neurons that communicate and work together for the body to heal. The neurons transporting electrical signals helping to move these electrical messages from neuron to neuron to heal and love the damaged body parts. See all this taking place while manifesting to fix and heal your damaged body or the damaged body of someone you love.

You have heard of people being able to walk when they were supposed to never move again. You have heard of them being able to create things that were unimaginable. Everything can be healed by manifesting it and willing it through love.

When you are manifesting, have fun with it. Have fun with your thoughts of what you are going to do with what you desire. Make it exciting and new. Manifest for a new job. See yourself walking into that new job that first day and feel the excitement of meeting your new coworkers. Feel and see yourself having fun, talking, laughing, and joking with them. See yourself at the new job where all your new friends and coworkers are loving and accepting of you.

THE SURPRISE PARTY

When manifesting, always be thankful for your desire as if it has already come to be. Say and write it as though it is in the present tense. Do not say, *I want a new bike* when manifesting. Say, *I love the new bike, it is so fun to ride, thank you.*

The first few times your manifestations come true; you might doubt how your manifestation came to be. It will be new to you and you will try to justify how it possibly happened and came to you. You might think, *the money for the bike came from a check from Andy that he should have paid me a year ago.* I am telling you, that check from Andy was not going to come if you had not manifested for the new bike. Stop those thoughts and turn them around, see it and believe it. Correct your false thoughts and apologize to yourself, your higher power, and the universe. You might think receiving your manifestation was only a coincidence. Stop those thoughts and know they are false. Your manifestation was all God, the universe, and you working together to bring it to be. It is not happenstance or coincidence. All three of you did this, starting with believing in your mind.

You are worthy of all good and there is plenty for all to go around. Do not sell yourself short of your desires, need, or wants. It is wrong programming to believe you only need the most basic of things to get by; there is plenty for all to enjoy in this beautiful world!

Your manifestations can take time. Be patient! They can take a year or even a few years, but I can tell you they will transpire over time. One day it will happen, and you may not recall that you had manifested it. If a manifestation has taken a long time, the manifestation might not be appropriate for you in your life any longer. That is ok; you can change it by giving thanks for it and sending it back to the universe. For instance, maybe you were looking for a new job and then sometime later after manifesting, you get a job offer. But now your current job starts to get better and everything has resolved and is working well in your profession. You do not need to yield to the manifestation. You can love it, thank it, and send it back to the universe. This is not being self-centered to your manifestation.

Teach this to your loved ones, both young and old. Teach them all the benefits of this beautiful insight. I can see it all happening one day, all beautiful human beings in this world manifesting together. What a beautiful sight I see. Let us all be together as one. Manifest for the good of all in this beautiful world. Let us all manifest for peace and no more world hunger in this beautiful world. There is plenty for all. Together it is happening, thank you!

18
Letting Go of the Pain

At this time in my life, I applied for a different position at the mental hospital I worked for, a position I still hold today. I had been working as a CNA for several years, learning a new love of humanity for these beautiful humans. I then changed positions and went into maintenance, doing repairs around the hospital for the next few years. I applied for a job in the Risk Management Department as the Risk Prevention Specialist and got the job! It entailed working in all areas of the hospital and making it safe for the patients, staff, and the buildings. A big part of my job is making sure my patients are safe which requires me to pre-inspect all patient areas looking for ways a patient could possibly harm themselves or others, a task I find ironic given my own trials and tendencies in life. I get to protect these beautiful men, women, and children from possibly harming themselves.

I was still doing a lot of exercising. I would go hours upon hours and day after day exercising. Even when I was training and exercising, I was praying and meditating. I would recite positive affirmations in my head the entire time I was working out. It was an enlightening time although I had a lot of commotion and sadness going on around me with my personal life. I would pray for hour and hours for my partner to be happy, but it was not helping.

Sadie and I were not doing well, and our marriage was failing. I was unhappy and trying to keep us together. And she was still in a deep depression. We decided that it was finally time to end our marriage for good. I moved out and there were words exchanged in frustration. We got the paperwork done through our attorneys and the divorce was final. We went our separate ways for good. I was devastated over everything we had gone through together. We still worked at the same facility, but we pretty much just avoided each other over the years, seeing each other only occasionally in passing. Sadie continued her life journey and I mine. I thank her for sharing her beautiful soul and her beautiful children with me. She is a wonderful mother and person. My life has been blessed by them.

During this time of my life was when I started to find the third healing insight. The third healing insight is letting go of pain. Your happiness and beauty are already deep within, to find it just remove the top layers of your trauma and pain. Through all tragedy, pain, and sadness the door of love will then be opened.

Many of us have traumas, sadness, or pain in our lives that we had no active role in, we were merely a recipient of these hardships. We need to let go of this pain. Ask yourself whether you have any anger toward anyone in your past; this could be a parent, family member, or it could even be someone you only met just for a moment in your past, like the other driver in a car accident. I encourage you to find it within you to let the sadness and pain go from these different traumatic events. When it came to the trauma and pain, I endured from my bicycle accident during the triathlon, I did not have any part in the accident but felt repercussions both emotionally and physically. The accident caused strain on my livelihood, my marriage, and many other areas that affected me and my family. To finally let go of the pain and trauma from the accident was a weight off my shoulders. To fully let go of the pain, I went back to the location of the accident. I shed some tears and had anxiety before I even got there. I wanted to turn the car around, but I drove on. I stayed at the intersection for some time, letting go of the pain, an experience that was both rewarding and finally freeing for me.

While working on this healing insight, I thought about an event that revealed to me how to let go of pain. This one event, which caused such pain, delayed my letting go for years. During my healing time, I was really working to let go of the pain from the past. I was praying and questioning when and where different events had occurred that decreased my happiness within. I needed to heal and let go of the past. I was trying to pin-point the pain and the events that had triggered it. One moment happened around the time my partner's son took his life. I knew this was a major moment in my life when I had lost all passion for life and had given up on myself. I still carried on living my life but was deeply unhappy. I knew it was not the passing of my partner's son, however, that did cause me other sadness and self-esteem problems. I knew there was something else that had occurred. I was really searching deep within!

One day while I was on my knees praying for answers, I was feeling quite frustrated, angry, and mad at life. I was just trying to get some peace. I was praying with all my soul, crying out to God, asking him, where were you when two little boys walked into their parents' bedroom as their father took his life? Where were you when my past partners endured sadness and pain and we ended our time together? Why didn't you help us fix our relationships? And then suddenly, out of the blue, I cried out, where were you when our power got turned off? After I said that, I stopped, wondering where that thought had come from. Why did I say that? It suddenly clicked in my mind. I said out loud, again, "Where were you when our power got turned off?" I thought back to when our power was shut off and realized, I had figured it out! I had found when I gave up my happiness! I had forgotten about this incident and did not comprehend how traumatizing it was for me. But looking back, I realize I can remember every part of the incident as though it was yesterday. Our minds play tricks on us, dismissing our pain and holding it in. Now getting this new understanding of what had taken place, I can remember the hardship that it caused me. This happened about a year after my partner's son had passed away. I was working a job making $9.41 an hour and my partner was not working much at that time due to the struggles she was having from her son's passing. We were financially struggling amid other problems. At that time, there were a lot of people out of work in our country due to the economic recession. My partner was gone that day when I arrived home from work; it was after-hours and school was out for all eight of our children who were out of the house playing at the time. I came home to find a big yellow tag hanging on my front door. The tag read, "Your power has been shut off due to nonpayment." It was a Friday afternoon just after 4 o'clock. I hurried and called the city power department, hoping to reach someone. I was emotional; it was terrible and embarrassing! I was pretty much already devastated and burnt out in life. I had everything against me! I had an entire family depending on power for cooking food, lights, etc. My partner was severely depressed and barely keeping it together. I also was sad from the tragedy and struggling and trying to keep everyone together! I was financially struggling doing all I could, working overtime shifts for any extra income. I was on hold waiting to speak to someone from the city power department regarding my bill. Finally, she picked up and I pleaded with her, asking if I can please just give them a hundred dollars toward my bill and then they could turn my power back on. The city worker told me they couldn't do that and that the only way to get the power back on was to pay the balance in full—and the only way to get it on for the weekend was to pay by 5 o'clock that day. I hung up the phone, walked into my bedroom, closed the door, and fell to my knees, sobbing. I screamed into my pillow, asking God, what do you want from me? What more can I do? I give up, I cannot do this anymore! I am doing everything I can to help my wife and keep our family together! Where are you!? I am dying here! I am dying inside! I am doing all I can to make extra money to pay the bills and it is not enough! I was sobbing, pleading and angry, yelling this into my pillow to God. I was devastated! At that moment, I gave up. I gave up on life. It was at that moment that I lost all my happiness within.

    I did not know the significance of this event and how devastating it was to me at that time. With everything else that was currently going wrong and had gone wrong in life, I did not realize that this moment had been the straw that broke the camel's back. I had all this devastation and sadness going on around me after my wife's son had passed away, but it was this small thing—getting the power shut off—that caused me to lose all happiness within. That small incident destroyed me! I was not happy for years and all those years I never knew why; I just knew I was no longer genuinely happy with life.

To let go of the pain, I had to mentally take myself back to this event and let the pain go. There were a lot of tears, but doing this made me look at life differently. It is not always the major traumas in your life that bring you down, it is sometimes the little things that take their toll on you. I was finally able to deal with it, work it out, and let the pain go.

After discovering the origin event for my pain, I was still struggling with completely letting go of it. I did not know what to do with the pain or how to release it. It was then that I had the insight to let it go into the universe and to a higher being. As I did earlier in my life when I asked God to take away my uncontrollable alcoholic cravings, I surrendered all my pain and sadness to a higher being. I encourage you to let your pain go out into the universe. Let your higher being take all your sadness and pain. I now surrender all my sadness and pain to Jehovah. I am thankful for this new peaceful insight and freedom within.

When you let go of the pain, you create space for a healthier love to enter your life. I want to encourage you to start looking deep into your past and letting go of your traumas. By doing this, you will open new doors to a blissful life. You are an amazing human being, and it is time to let go of all your past sufferings.

During my time of letting go of pain, trauma, and resentment, I discovered that I had distrusted most everyone I knew. I started to see how my distrust of others impacted me and how it weighed on my life. It was not until I had come to this healing time that I noticed I was constantly walking around with a big chip on my shoulder. I believed that everyone had an agenda to take advantage of me or my loved ones. I started to look at this behavior to figure out where this distrust originated from. After really searching my past and the deep feelings of distrust, I identified some events in my childhood that caused these beliefs to start. Certain things happened that, as a young child, made me feel powerless and distrustful of others. One specific incident stuck out in my mind: a family friend had taken advantage of my mother by charging her too much for some work that he had done. I remember overhearing him talk to another gentleman saying he was going to over-charge her. He then saw that I had heard the conversation and, knowing he was caught, just kind of laughed it off. I was a young boy and I recall wishing I were bigger and older so I could stand up to him and do something to protect my mother. I remember feeling so defeated!

At a young age, I began living as if I could never take or receive anything from anyone, even my closest loved ones, for fear they would take advantage of me or use it against me. I also felt I needed to protect everyone from possibly getting taken advantage of. Just as I felt I had to protect my mother; I spent my life feeling the need to protect everyone I loved from possibly being taken advantage of by others. I carried a lot of weight on my shoulders protecting everyone I loved from any pain.

    I grew up believing that if I took anything from anyone, I owed them. I carried this resentment into all parts of my life—my relationships, my job, and even with my close friends. I always gave, never received, and because I thought to receive would be to put my vulnerability out there. I believed I needed to constantly protect myself and others, a belief which kept me distant from everyone. It's almost amusing that I felt this belief so strongly when I love everyone with all my heart and soul. Now that I saw how often I thought and acted on this uncertainty; I knew it was time to fix my problem. I really had to start looking at people differently and finding a deeper love for them. I let go of the pain and changed my mindset, looking at them as who they truly were, as the souls that they were before they came here for their earthly experience. I tried looking at the true love and kindness within their hearts. I have heard some people do this by looking at them as they do Christ.

    Letting your pain go does not mean the pain never existed, it just means that the pain no longer controls your life. I encourage you to dig deep within and let go of all your past pain and traumas. You will find a freedom that you did not know existed.

19

Loving Yourself

Life was changing for me and one day I met a beautiful woman, Kelly. She is probably one of the most life-changing souls I have ever met. Kelly is truly an angel from God! And she is gorgeous. She is an amazing mother that has made this world a better place. We had the same beliefs and dreams. She took the broken soul I was and tried to give me life. I felt a love from her I had never felt before. I had given up on love and myself and was filled with sadness. I believed I was not a good person, but rather a failure, a bad father, and a mean person. This beautiful angel and friend took me in and loved me. We became best friends.

My best friend and I spent a beautiful two years in love together; we enjoyed each other so much. She was so kind to me and my family, a kindness I didn't know existed. She tried to lift my soul when I was down. When I met her, I was at another rock bottom low and my self-esteem had tanked. My negative inner voices had taken over and they were winning. They were telling me I was not good enough for her and that I was not worthy of her love. They told me I was worthy of no one's love. They told me I needed to take my life. They told me my four boys were now all raised, and they did not need me.

I felt no need to go onward. I decided I needed to break things off with her. I was struggling so hard with my self-esteem and doubts—I knew I needed to get some personal help. I needed to let her go because I knew I could not give her the love she deserved when I did not love myself. I had finally had enough of all the negative voices going on in my mind. It was time to beat them for good, reprogram and be done with them controlling my life. I knew it was time to unravel all the damage from my lifetime. I broke up with her, and we went our separate ways. It was one of the hardest things I have ever done. I had a lot of tears and sadness. I was leaving an amazing soul, mother, and friend! It was so hard to leave this beautiful best friend of mine. She loved me and I did her. Kelly's love made me see I needed to find peace within and learn to love myself. I look back at it and this is when my life started changing. The first time I hit rock bottom in my life was from the drinking and self-destruction of being an alcoholic. This time in my life, I hit a rock bottom from my self-esteem and negative thoughts. I knew I needed to change myself. I had everything I ever wanted, and all my needs were met, but I was not doing well. I had so much sadness internally. I believed that I had been completely at fault in all my relationships, just as I believed that I was completely at fault for my father's death when I was a young boy. I have done a lot of research on the different problems I endured in my life and learned that a common characteristic of people with abandonment issues is taking all the blame on themselves. I was taking every past relationship and life trial I had endured and blaming it all on myself. I ended my relationship with Kelly and felt heartbroken. I thank Kelly for the love she gave to me. She taught me a new kind of love that I didn't know existed. I am a better person and I know a superior kind of love because of her.

You can have beautiful people around you and everything you ever wanted, but if you do not have love for yourself, you have nothing.

This leads me into the second part of the healing insight of forgiveness. I talked about the first part earlier in the book regarding forgiving my father and his choices. The second part of the forgiveness process is forgiving yourself for any difficulty and pain you caused others. To forgive yourself for pain you have caused others, ask yourself whether you really forgive yourself. Forgiving yourself can be difficult, oftentimes more difficult than forgiving others. This was a big one for me. One area I worked on was letting go of my sadness, pain, and ownership from my unsuccessful relationships. This was me also taking ownership for the pain I may have caused my significant other in any of my past relationships. This was me finally forgiving myself. I had a lot of guilt over the years from the pain I may have caused. While I was doing a lot of work on healing myself within, I was also working with my therapist at the time. Like I did with the first part of the forgiveness insight of letting go of the pain regarding my father, I was encouraged to write an apology letter for my part in my past relationships. I took that advice and, by doing this exercise, I was not only able to end a lot of the personal heartache for my part in the hardships of my relationships but also able to reconcile with some of my former significant others. By doing this, I was able to start healing from the past that I had never completely healed from. The peace and forgiveness I felt which allowed for healing to begin was overwhelming. I believe this is a good practice for anyone to do, if possible, a few years after the end of a difficult relationship. Doing this some time after a relationship has ended allows both parties to have time to let go of resentments, anger, and sadness felt toward the other person. It would be helpful for so many people to write a letter like this or even meet up to apologize for their part in the unsuccessful relationship. I wish everyone could and would do this and let the past and their hard feelings go in hopes to possibly forgive. I was blessed that some of my past relationships allowed this to happen. This was a beautiful time for apologizing and forgiving each other, and then I was able to start the healing process. From there, we were able to let go of a lot of past sufferings and wished each other well on our life adventures. Writing a letter to my past relationships was a good start for me in forgiving and letting go of my past.

You can forgive someone without the need to write them or talk to them. You can just forgive them within in your heart and mind and then let them go in peace. By healing yourself you are healing generations. This is a lot of work and I am talking a lot of work! It took me a lot of time and patience to find forgiveness for the many traumas in my life. It was a beautiful, forgiving experience.

After this rock bottom time in my life and knowing I needed to fix myself was when I learned the fourth and most important healing insight of them all: loving yourself.

I spent my entire life not loving myself. I have always placed my desires, comforts, and happiness second or even last to everyone else's. At this time in my life, I started searching within to find my happiness. I was quite fascinated by how far I had come in my life after having given up on myself. I want to share the techniques I used in my healing journey in the hopes that they encourage you to look within and find love for yourself. If you have no fears or self-doubt, this section of the book may not apply, although I believe we can all benefit from more self-love.

I am going to ask you do to a lot of self-evaluation. Self-healing requires a tremendous amount of action and willingness to go beyond your normal way of living. I hope you will dig deep within and evaluate your love for yourself and for others. As you are searching, you might even have to go to war with yourself and confront your deepest, darkest fears. When you are digging into your past, I encourage you to identify any self-doubts and fears you may have and where those might have originated. Look at every aspect of your life, your career, family, and relationships. Think back to when and if you ever stopped believing in yourself. Your fears and doubts are the source of your loss of love for yourself. You should never place yourself second. Let me repeat that, you should never place yourself second! In my case, I knew deep down that I was not happy. I had not been genuinely happy with myself for years or even most of my life. I wanted to find out when I lost my love for myself.

There are two parts to the fourth and final healing insight: loving yourself above all which is the highest form of love and knowing you are worthy of love, the second-highest form. Choosing to love yourself and accepting that you are worthy of love are the most important decisions you will make in your life. We start to lose these two insights throughout our life, whether due to mental or physical trauma caused by ourselves or by others. We bring judgment on ourselves due to "wrong" life choices and begin to mentally abuse ourselves. Mental abuse from others, whether due to growing up in a dysfunctional family or entering a dysfunctional relationship and self-harming addictions, whether due to alcohol, drugs, food, etc., all contribute to our loss of self-love. Learning to love yourself and knowing you are worthy of love is achieved by having confidence within ourselves and knowing you are safe.

Let us start with the first part: loving yourself. I would like you to really think and ask yourself these questions: Do I love myself above all? Do I love myself deep down to my core? Do I feel guilty if I put my needs first? In what ways do I show love for myself? How do I respond to someone telling me I'm not good enough? Next, look at yourself in a mirror completely undressed; can you tell yourself you love yourself and you are beautiful? Are you embarrassed of your looks? Can you say to yourself; I am stunning and beautiful? I encourage you to ask yourself these questions and ponder the answers.

As I have grown older, I have learned that self-love is the most important power there is in our lives. We face many different trials and tend to forget who the most important player is on the team during the process. We lose ourselves in the face of traumas, in our relationships when we constantly try to please the other person, and in our professional lives trying to please management. And we lose ourselves in our daily lives simply with all the run-around. It is up to you to be healthy and love yourself; no one can rescue you from a lack of self-love. It is 100% your responsibility. Loving yourself first is all up to you.

No partner in any relationship can give you self-love. This is where relationships tend to fail. If you do not and cannot learn to love yourself first, how can you expect to give or receive love in your relationship? It is not your responsibility to make the other person happy; it is your responsibility to love yourself first and be happy. In doing so, your positive, loving energy will resonate around you, teaching others to love themselves first. If you love yourself first, your loved ones will see this and gravitate toward you. And this might take time. But if you keep being happy and loving yourself first, after time your loved ones will learn from you and attract a stronger love for themselves. Have you ever heard someone tell you that their childhood memories are of their parents or parent were always yelling or unhappy? The fact is that their parent or parents did not have love for themselves. If the parent or parents would have had love for themselves first, they would have transferred their love for themselves to all the loved ones around them. There would have been unity within the family.

If you are not happy within and you have exhausted all other options to find self-love, then it is time to take care of yourself and do what is best for you. This is not selfish! No teaching suggests that you should take all love and energy from yourself and dedicate it to others, depleting your own self-love. Living this way will ensure failure.

You might be feeling a bit of resistance to this insight of self-love. Questioning your relationship? It is selfish to love myself first! My relationship will fail if I do not take care of my partner! No, it will fail if you do not take care of yourself and love yourself first. If your relationship is to the point where it is failing and you have exhausted all resources including therapy and self-help, then it is time to take care of yourself and your needs. This is not selfish. God and the universe do not want you to be unhappy or without self-love. Feeling otherwise is the result of past wrong programming which taught you to believe that loving one's self is selfish. This goes for all areas of your life: your profession, family, relationship, and well-being; never allow anyone to slowly bring you down. You would not want anyone you love to have a lack of love for themselves. So why would you allow this to happen to yourself?

This was the hardest insight for me to learn and embrace; it took me 45 years to learn. I know my life would have been completely different if I had learned this healing insight at a younger age. My life choices might have had a completely different outcome.

Looking back, I always had love for all human beings, but I forgot love for one person: myself. One of the biggest steps toward learning to love yourself is letting go of the judgment of ourselves for what we call "wrong life choices." There are no wrong choices on our life journey, only opportunities for learning. Stop the judgment, guilt, and shame. Again, you did no wrong! Stop any judgment of others if you have done so. We are all on our own life journeys. We are on a learning journey to become masters of loving ourselves and others. If you have hurt others in the past, forgive yourself and learn to love differently and healthily. Greed, anger, or any ill will toward another comes back to that individual not loving themselves. The underlying reason you may have hurt others was because you did not love yourself first.

Take the time to forgive yourself if you feel you have transgressions in the past; know that you did all you could do with what you were taught and what you knew at the time. Know that you tried your hardest with what you were given and then forgive yourself and others. Finally, look at yourself and know you are a success. Let go of your past and have no regrets, then realize what an amazing, loving human being you are. Recognize that you did it and you succeeded! You are alive today and you are beautiful!

How do you learn to love yourself? First, you make it a goal and write it down on a piece of paper. I hope you write it for everyone to see, but if not, that is also ok. Just writing it down as you work on this is a good first step.

When writing down the first healing insight as a goal, you might also write, "I am safe, and I love myself" to start putting it into your mind. Write it hundreds of times if needed. As you are writing this, I encourage you to constantly tell yourself throughout the day and every day from here on out that you are safe and that you love yourself. Really drill it into your mind that you are a magnificent, intelligent, beautiful person; believe it and know it.

As you learn to trust yourself and continue to tell yourself you are safe and love yourself, you are already doing amazing work, changing all those years of bad programming. I had lots of years of wrong programming, 45 to be exact. I doubted myself and I did not think I could ever love myself. But it can be done, and it is possible. Believe it, live it, know it, and your thinking process will change.

Next is caring for yourself. I challenge you to step outside your comfort zone during this step. Treat yourself like you are dating yourself for the first time. Buy yourself roses; you deserve it! Be the most romantic person there ever was to yourself. Take yourself on a trip alone, if possible. Be alone, if you can, every day for even just 15 minutes. While alone, do and say nice things to yourself. Build assurance within yourself while being alone. Let all your doubts and fears go during this time. Being alone for even a small amount of time every day is healthy and is ok. Do not be afraid to be alone. You do not need anyone else to protect you. Remind yourself you are safe and strong.

I recommend exercising, going on a walk, or hiking in nature. Nature is a great teacher to help you learn to love yourself. If possible, get a massage and pamper yourself—you deserve it! Build yourself up by eating and being healthy. Try looking into a mirror daily while undressed and tell yourself you love yourself and you are beautiful. Remind yourself there is no shame in your beauty while being completely undressed. Some of us have been taught to cover ourselves up, implanting the idea in our minds that we all must have the same body or feel shame in our own. There is no shame in your naked self—that shame is simply the result of outdated beliefs. If you are ashamed of your naked self, how do you expect someone else to want to be with you undressed? Show yourself respect; you are beautiful naked! Only allow those who are worthy to see your naked beauty. We are all beautiful naked. Allow confidence to build within you that is unbreakable and unstoppable. Love yourself, treat yourself well, and remind yourself you are the queen or king of this amazing life journey. Love yourself above all because you're with this lovely person for the rest of your life.

As you practice these steps and implement them into your life, one day you will suddenly start to see it: you will notice small amounts of confidence and love coming into your heart. You will start to realize what an amazing job you have done in your life considering all that you have been through. You will realize that you are and have always been a good person who is lovable. This is self-love. For the rest of your life, please never stop practicing the healing insight of self-love.

I started to search deep into my past and worked on letting go of a lot of personal sadness I had endured that resulted in the loss of love for myself. This was a very spiritual time in my life and a lot of new spiritual growth was taking place. I worked on forgiving my father's legacy for leading me to my past unsuccessful relationships. I started to finally put an end to all my bad thoughts and beliefs about myself. These are just some of the insights I gained during this time. I am hopeful that my own journey will encourage you to start yours and to channel new ways to let go of your fears and doubts. I want you to know you are beautiful! The healing journey never ends, and our success always continues.

As I was learning the healing insight of loving myself, I had to do a lot of reprogramming and change my mindset. While I was working to find a love for myself, I was speaking with a therapist about my new outlook and the new love for myself that I was finding within. I was telling her how thankful I was to God and my unconditional love for God. I have always been thankful and had an immense love for my higher being ever since I was able to quit drinking. My therapist said to me, "You know what you have done is you have built your home upside down." I asked what she meant. "You built your home upside down with your experiences from your life. You put the walls, roof, and everything on the ground first," she explained. "You then laid the foundation, which is God, on top of all the walls and roof." I paused and I thought about it. She was right!

Later, after our discussion, I laughed out loud at this metaphor. She was right!

God is the foundation of all our lives. Looking at our life as a home, Jehovah is the foundation. This foundation has deep footings, concrete footings with steel and rebar, and massive concrete walls all tied together with metal rebar. All the rebar and metal are binding everything together solid and tight. This is the hardest mixed concrete there is, mixed precisely with all the correct elements. And it has been laid down with perfection. That is God, he is our foundation!

From a solid foundation, we start to build our home. I started to see my home as my love for myself in my mind; I was thinking, yes, I will build these beautiful walls, big, strong walls for stability in my love for myself! I started to build the home and add the roof. Was the roof where a relationship could be a part of my life? Where would a relationship be a part of the home and loving myself, knowing I am worthy of love? At first, I was thinking a part of the outside of the structure. But I realized a relationship would be the roof, the kind of roof that pulls everything together and keeps everything rain tight.

Not long after this insight about the beautiful home, a different insight came to me. Suddenly, I saw it in my mind—I had some incorrect parts to my home and my love for myself. Everything regarding the foundation—God—was correct. Then I realized that this is where the changes start. This home is not just any strong home symbolizing my self-love. This home is a massive, beautiful log cabin! It has the oldest, grandest, immense logs. These logs are going to stand the test of time and are stacked together tight and sound. The logs and beams are driven together with strong, plated steel straps tying it all together. This magnificent log cabin that is I has strong wooden beams and a roof made of the finest wood on the inside and a solid, rain-tight metal exterior that can withstand the most brutal storms and heaviest of snow loads. All the logs are stained and lacquered with the strongest protective coating made. I, being this massive, sound log cabin, can withstand any type of elements i.e., fears and doubts. What a gorgeous, beautiful log cabin it is that symbolizes me and the love I have for myself.

Now this is where all the other beauty comes into the cabin. The beautiful relationship is the warmth of the cabin; it is a vast, wood-burning stove keeping it cozy and filling it with warmth and love. And all the other inside beauty of the home is a family filling it with the softest, warmest love. That is my new outlook on life and the love I have for myself. We are as we see ourselves in our own mind.

I encourage you to change your mindset and reprogram your thinking to build a new and stronger love for yourself as a beautiful home as I did. Make your home as amazing as you are. Give your home the finest love for yourself as you are deserving of. Before this healing time in my life, when I was at an ultimate low in terms of self-love and self-esteem, I was working hard to end the negative thoughts once and for all. I had finally had enough. I was having thoughts of death that I always had along with suicidal thoughts. All these thoughts were taking up every ounce of energy I had. The thoughts were firing in my mind every hour, minute, second as they had done most my life. I know there are others out there who deal with this in their life and I hope you get some professional help and never give in to the wrong voices.

As I was working to reprogram and stop all my negative feelings and thoughts, I had begun implementing the fourth healing insight. This therapist I was seeing at the time simply said, "Now you are finding some peace on this healing journey even though these bad thoughts still appear in your mind occasionally." She encouraged me to reprogram my mind to think about them in a different way. "When one comes to you, stop what you are doing and stop the thoughts before they end." I had been doing this and I was working hard to catch and stop these bad thoughts, never letting them finish, reprogramming, and never letting them run free in my mind as they had done throughout my life. She encouraged me to take those thoughts and give them to God in my mind. I was already trying to do this with the reprogramming. She then told me to make a story of it and see it differently. She told me to take those negative thoughts and make them into a big rock. Then take that rock and throw it into a pond. Now around that beautiful pond are all your loved ones and all the beautiful people that you have ever loved in your life. Everyone you have ever loved is around this pond. As you throw that rock, it lands in the water and it sinks.

This was a beautiful way to reprogram my wrong negative thoughts. As I did with the log cabin metaphor, after thinking of it for some time, I added more to the story to make it personally fit me. In my mind, I now see myself taking the wrong, nasty thought I had and personally handing it to God. I place it into his hands. I then love Jehovah and thank him. Jehovah then turns that terrible thought into a rock. Next, he hands the rock back to me. I then throw the rock as far as I can into a beautiful pond. Sometimes God hands me back a big rock due to the intensity of the thought. The rock hits the water with a big splash and sinks all the way to the bottom of the pond to never be seen again. Ripples form from the rock hitting the water, sending small waves all the way out to the shorelines of the pond. All around this beautiful pond are all the people I have ever loved and will ever love. The ripples represent the love from my heart and soul being sent out to all my loved ones. That negative thought is turned into love and it literally feeds love to my loved ones. I started to practice this reprograming in my mind, and I started to believe it and see this in my head. If a terrible thought of death or suicide comes to my mind, I catch the thought and stop what I am doing and replay this beautiful scenario in my head. There have been times I have even had to stop the car and pull over to think of the healing insight scenario in my mind to stop the negative thought.

I put this story into my mind, and it started to work. This was a big life-changing moment for me. I give you these examples of reprogramming negative thoughts to encourage you to take these different ideas and work them into your life to stop any unwanted thoughts you are possibly having trouble with. Make up your own story and implement it into your healing journey. It all begins with your thoughts and if you give a negative thought any power it becomes powerful. If you instantly stop the negative thought, it becomes powerless and is nothing.

I pray that you do not deal with any terrible thoughts, however I am sure there are many of you out there dealing with them. These can be addictions, negative self-thoughts, or negative thoughts toward someone else. I want to remind you that you are beautiful and loving. And please get some professional help if you are struggling with any harmful thoughts. I hope you can take these ideas and make your own scenarios and stories to replace those bad, unwanted thoughts you may be having. Please reprogram your beautiful mind by stopping all negative thoughts and turn them into a beautiful new love for yourself.

If I had not evaluated my programmed beliefs and been open-minded to experiencing the many wonderful cultures I have, I would have never reached this blissful stage in my life. Reprogramming my beliefs has brought me a new, higher form of self-love. I encourage you to investigate different ways of your life, different philosophies, and different understandings. Please step outside of your programmed beliefs and experience all the beautiful different cultures. You can still follow one path that you believe in as the truth. That is beautiful and that makes you perfect in your own way. But know that there is truth and loveliness in all the paths we wander and as you learn of them, just simply add them to your current path. May you find courage to break the unhealthy patterns in your life and fine a new healthy love for yourself.

Let us now talk about the second part of this insight, knowing you are worthy of love. Ask yourself these questions: Do I feel I am worthy of the utmost love? Do I know that I only deserve the grandest love from others? No matter the answers you tell yourself, I want you to know that you *do* deserve the utmost love and respect from all other human beings. I want you to know you are deserving of only the grandest love from others. As you work on loving yourself and building your confidence, this next part will start to come naturally. Loving yourself is key to feeling worthy of love, something that is often difficult for those of us with unloving upbringings. I did not believe that I was worthy of love.

Just as you practiced with the first part of this insight, you will also need to constantly remind yourself you are worthy of being loved. I encourage you to also write this down as a goal. Write: I am worthy of kindness and being loved by others. Let me say this again, you are worthy of kindness and of being loved! This will help you to set expectations for only the most genuine love from others. Never accept less for yourself and never allow yourself to feel unloved. Program this into your mind. Believe you are worthy of being loved and deserving of only the highest form of love and kindness from all others.

It took a lot of time and reprogramming for me to learn this insight. I still work on it every day, but I love myself first. The fact is, you are a loving, strong, empowered human being. Self-growth is not always easy. You are an amazing person with all the potential in the world to change your life and others.

This powerful insight is the most important to teach your loved ones, children, family, and friends. I look back at my time raising my children and I always taught them to chase their dreams and that they could have and become whatever they desired. But I forgot to teach them the most important insight of all: to love themselves first. I am working on teaching my children this now in their adult lives. I do not see a lot of other parents teaching their young child to love themselves above all. I always hear parents and society telling children to always chase their dreams, but self-love does not seem to be taught or as important. When teaching self-love, also teach them that they are worthy of love. Anyone you teach these insights to, young or old, will benefit in their relationships and life experiences.

Remember that we are all on this beautiful, loving journey together. Let us help each other out by teaching others these beautiful insights. Remind anyone you might meet, even someone you bump into at the store, that they are loved and to love themselves first.

Conclusion

You are a spiritual giant within. The key is to tap into your spiritual side and find your true self. I encourage you to learn and explore these insights and unleash that spiritual giant. I manifest that these insights will give you a new insightful foundation. Again, this is only the beginning. There is more out there; please find it within! There is no end to practicing these wonderful insights—they go on forever.

As you get up every morning and go about your day, I want you to have a new love for yourself that is enhanced 100-fold. I manifest and know that these healing and discovery insights will help you in every part of your life. They will help you enhance your spiritual relationship or finally discover that spiritual relationship that you did not believe existed. They will help you in landing that job of a lifetime or getting the promotion at work. Everything you ever dreamed of is yours if you believe in these insights.

You are a beautiful soul that gives light to this world. Love within and love yourself first, then reach out and love all others. We are all on our own healing and discovery journey to find our true selves. We are all trying to become better people and trying to love more every day. You are a light in this world and the light of God.

Your story is also the greatest love story ever told! The best is yet to come and is a new, exciting, unwritten story. And

LOVE YOURSELF

I know what is to come for you will be even more beautiful than what has already transpired. I am excited for you to continue the next chapter of your great love story. Every day can be a new surprise party; it is your choice, make it.

Made in the USA
Monee, IL
14 July 2022